Marathoning, Start to Finish

5th Edition
Copyright (c) 2004-2014 wY'east Consulting, All Rights reserved

By Patti and Warren Finke
Supplemental Training by Janet Hamilton
Illustrations by Clive Davies

Published by wY'east Consulting
22066-A SW Grahams Ferry Road, Tualatin, OR 97062

www.TeamOregon.com

Contents

Introduction..6

Starting Out...8

Training Principles..12
   Marathon Physiology...13
      Energy Sources..15
      Muscles..19
      VO2 max..21
      Endurance..22
      Efficiency...23
      Central Governor or Anticipatory Regulation....................................24
   Keys to Success..25
      Hard/Easy Cycles and Progressive Overload..................................26
      Specificity..27
      Injury Prevention Techniques..28

Base Building...36
   Plans, Paces and Progressions...37
      Novice Marathon Basebuilding..42
      Beginning Marathon Basebuilding...43
      Recreational Marathon Basebuilding...44
      Intermediate Marathon Basebuilding...45
      Advanced Marathon Basebuilding...46
      Getting Out The Door...47

Sharpening..50
   Maximizing Performance...51
      Novice Marathon Sharpening...57
      Beginning Marathon Sharpening..58
      Recreational Marathon Sharpening..59
      Intermediate Marathon Sharpening..60
      Advanced Marathon Sharpening..61
   Psychological Preparation..62
      Goals - Setting Yourself up to Win...64
      Vision - Making Things Happen..66
      Self-control - Dealing With Challenges and Focusing Energy.............69
      Relaxation..71
      Focus...72
      Achieving "The Zone"...73
      Quick Reference to Psychological Training Techniques...................74
   Peaking...75

- Race Preparation...78
  - Tapering...79
    - Novice Marathon Tapering...80
    - Beginning Marathon Tapering...81
    - Recreational Marathon Tapering...82
    - Intermediate Marathon Tapering...83
    - Advanced Marathon Tapering...84
  - Carbohydrate Loading...85
  - Planning Your Race...88
- Racing...94
  - Final Preparation...95
  - Race Tactics...98
- Recovery...104
  - After Your Race...105
    - Novice Marathon Recovery...109
    - Beginning Marathon Recovery...110
    - Recreational Marathon Recovery...111
    - Intermediate Marathon Recovery...112
    - Advanced Marathon Recovery...113
- Aids to Performance...114
  - Supplemental Training...115
    - Flexibility...116
    - Strength Training...125
  - Food and Performance...141
    - How Much to Eat...142
    - What Nutrients to Eat...143
    - What Foods to Eat...152
    - When to Eat...155
  - Ergogenic Aids...160
    - Nutritional Aids...161
    - Physiological Aids...163
    - Pharmacological Aids...165
  - Running in Temperature Extremes...168
    - Performance in Temperature Extremes...169
    - Heat Illnesses...170
    - Heat Acclimatization...172
    - Fluid and Electrolyte Replacement...174
    - Hyponatremia...175
    - Running in the Cold...176
  - Safety Concerns...178

- Appendices 180
  - Example Training Log 180
  - Pace Tables 182
  - Heart Rate Tables 190
  - References 196
  - About This Book 200
  - The Authors 201

Introduction

The marathon race has been traced to 776 BC and the races held at the ancient Greek Olympic Games. The games came to an end in 349 AD when the Christian Emperor of Rome banned the Olympic Festival as a relic of paganism. In the following centuries, the glorious deeds of the athletes and the noble spirit of the Olympic competition were not forgotten.

The father of the modern Olympics was Baron Pierre de Coubertin, who dreamed of an athletic competition worthy of the name Olympics that would bring together the best athletes of all nations of the world for a series of contests dedicated to the highest ideals of amateurism, brotherhood and peace. In 1894 Coubertin arranged a meeting of representatives of dozens of nations and the International Olympic Committee was formed to stage the first Olympics of the modern age to be held in Athens in the spring of 1896. One of the events to be included was a race designed to retrace the steps of the Greek soldier who in 490 BC, after helping the Athenians trounce the invading Persians at the Battle of Marathon, ran 25 miles from Marathon to Athens to proclaim the news. When he arrived he gasped "Rejoice we have conquered", then died on the spot. The Greek historian Herodotus, who did not identify the runner, recorded this event.

On April 10, 1896, 25 runners heard the gun go off at Marathon for the Olympic race and started the 25 mile course over rock strewn roads. More than 60,000 spectators were in the Athens stadium and another 60,000 were on the hills watching the games and waiting for the marathoners to arrive. The favored Greek runners were well off the pace for the first half of the race, but one, Spiridon Loues, steadily moved up through the slowing pack starting at about the 15 mile point. He caught the leader, the Australian Flack. They raced side by side until Flack collapsed at mile 23. With the stadium in sight, Loues ran down a path cleared by the police through a crowd that was showering him with flower petals. The Greek spectators went wild with enthusiasm as their runner won the race. This race was the beginning of the modern marathon. The marathon has been an event in each Olympics since then and in 1984 included a women's race for the first time. The official distance was changed to 26 miles 385 yards at the London Olympics in 1908. The extra distance was added so that the royal family could watch the start from Windsor Castle. The first American marathon was sponsored by the Boston Athletic Association in 1897 and the event has grown tremendously ever since.

From Start to Finish
Every marathon starts long before the runners merge behind the starting line waiting for the gun to go off. A commitment by the runner to do the actual training required to cover the miles is the real beginning. The marathon does not finish when the runner crosses the line. It finishes only after the runner recovers, is able to enjoy the magnitude of his/her accomplishment and is motivated to set new running goals.

This book approaches marathoning with an emphasis on efficiency of training and prevention of injury. The training program described is one that the authors have developed and used personally for over 35 years they have been running and competing. 30 years of experience coaching runners of all abilities have refined it. It combines thousands of miles of trial and error experience and the results of the latest exercise physiology research. Predictably, exercise physiology reinforced what the authors had, for the most part, learned the hard way. The program is the philosophical basis of the Portland Marathon Clinic, a 6 month series of lectures and training runs co-directed by the authors (Patti and Warren), DeeAnn Dougherty and Katie Hunter. The clinic has successfully guided thousands of runners to successful marathon completions. The main goal of this book and the Clinic is to make the marathon experience as rewarding and enjoyable as possible for all participants, whether novice or seasoned veterans.

Starting Out

Are You Ready?

How can you determine if you are ready to start training for the marathon? Marathoning is not for the beginning runner. You should have been running for at least 6 months and be running at least 8-12 miles per week if you want to run a marathon 6 months from now. If you already have a good mileage base or have run previous marathons, then you're definitely ready to begin a training program designed to help you reach your top performance.

You should already have a good level of fitness and have consulted with your physician concerning any medical problems.

The training programs described in this book are conservative with emphasis on injury prevention and adequate rest. They stress ENDURANCE by using long slow runs done at 80% effort. Runners left to their own devices often train at 90% which limits the length of their runs and makes them much less enjoyable and less specific for training the energy systems needed for endurance running.

We heartily concur with the recommendation of the American Academy of Pediatrics that children, before puberty, should not run the marathon. We've seen too many children suffer psychological burnout and physical problems to feel otherwise.

There is no difference in marathon training between men and women except when women are pregnant. Fitness running (30 minutes, 3 - 5 times/week) may be appropriate for pregnant runners; more exercise than this may be harmful to the baby. Pregnancy is not the time to increase or start a new exercise program.

Are there special considerations for the older runner? Clive Davies, a friend and this book's illustrator, was still setting national age group records at the marathon and lesser distances when he turned 70. Studies of middle aged marathoners showed that they compared favorably with runners in their 20's in high aerobic capacity, high efficiency of energy, low percentage of body fat and ability to exercise at a high percentage of their aerobic capacity. In the late 1980s, the world best for the marathon was run by Carlos Lopes at age 38. Although you may still perform well, as you get older you may find that you need more time to recover. You may have to run fewer miles and run those miles at a slower pace. Supplemental and cross training may also be more important.

Goal Setting

The first step in any program is to define goals. The term goals is used in the plural sense because a series of goals should be set: long, medium and short range. A long range goal may be to finish your first marathon, or to improve your time from a previous marathon best. Shorter term goals may include running several 20 mile training runs and increasing your weekly training mileage.

The value of goals results from the fact that the higher standards you set for yourself, the higher your attainment. The setting of performance goals does not in itself produce achievement. Achievement is driven by self-confidence. The motivational effect of reaching goals is to increase self-confidence. Added self-confidence drives you to attempt progressively more difficult goals. Success then results from seeking out and conquering challenges by achieving a series of goals that are optimal for you, neither too difficult nor too easy.

Commitment

The setting of goals must be accompanied by commitment. In life, to excel you must use your abilities to the fullest capacity. To excel in the marathon, you must be physically and psychologically fit. You must believe in your own capabilities and fully commit yourself to their fullest development. Commitment is a major key to the psychological attributes necessary for excellence. Peak performance comes from assuming active responsibility for your own success. We can show you the necessary tools, but you must use them. The level of your commitment to the marathon is your choice.

Volition or willpower is the core of the self. Willpower decides what is to be done, applies the means to do the task and persists in the task in the face of all obstacles. Learn to identify volition by identifying your personal needs and the experiences that strengthen you. Volition affects mental performance, thoughts, feelings and physical parameters such as strength, responsiveness and the desire to succeed.

A part of commitment is "mission" or your personal reasons for pursuing a particular goal. While your goal may be to finish, your mission may be to be in command of your body and push it to its limits.

Outlining a Plan

One way to help achieve a day to day level of commitment is to formulate a plan and keep track of your progress. A training plan is a set of long range, medium range and daily goals. Start now by writing down your long range goal (i.e. running a marathon in some time). In the following chapters we'll show you what medium range goals (training milestones) will support this. If you follow the points set out here, you will be able to devise a week by week, day by day training plan. This technique will yield a systematic approach to achieving your long range goal via a series of small and achievable steps leading from where you are now to where you want to go. Each step can be used to assess progress toward your long range goal.

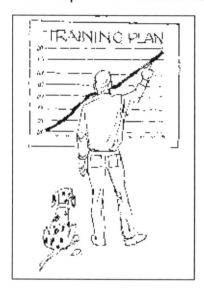

Training Principles

Marathon Physiology

Physiologic principles and adaptations form the basis for marathon training requirements. There are two basic principles that underlie all types of athletic training: overload and specificity.

Overload

Overload means exercising at a level that causes the body to make specific adaptations to function more efficiently. Overload does not mean over training. Think of a rubber band - as more pull is applied it stretches more and becomes easier to stretch, but too much pull can cause it to snap. To keep the runner from breaking (i.e., becoming injured, ill or psychologically burned out), overload must always be used in conjunction with rest. Overload and rest form the basis for what is known as the "hard/easy" training approach. This technique uses variations in frequency, intensity and duration to achieve cycles of overload and rest. Frequency is how often you run, intensity is the pace at which the workout is conducted and duration is the time spent on an individual run. In a program of increasing mileage or of building basic endurance, "hard" may be a long slow run while "easy" may be a shorter distance run at the same effort. For the experienced runner with an established mileage base, "hard" might be a shorter workout of increased intensity such as hill work, fartlek or some kind of interval training. After a hard workout, rest or an easy workout is important because it allows the muscles and other tissues a chance to rebuild and adapt to the stress. This is the basis of overload training.

Specificity

Specificity refers to adaptations of both metabolic and physiologic systems, depending on the type of overload used. Specific exercise brings about changes in those systems used in that particular exercise. Obviously, running is the specific training for running. Different adaptations result from different kinds of running using variations of frequency, intensity, duration and terrain to utilize different sources of energy and different neuromuscular facilitation of muscle groups. This is where long term goal setting is so important: you need a running program designed for the specific type of races you want to run. This approach will assist you to maximize performance and eliminate wasted effort. Specific endurance training with its resultant physiologic adaptations is essential for marathons.

Performance

The largest contributor to athletic performance is heredity. The heredity curve is bell shaped with very few individuals at either end and most of us in the middle. While you cannot change your heredity, you can maximize performance by using effective training based on some knowledge of the body's physiology.

Next to heredity, the most important aspect of human performance is the ability of the body to efficiently utilize it's fuel resources. The effects of training on the major elements of the pulmonary and cardiovascular systems and on the profusion and structure of muscles, mitochondria, enzymes and other factors all control the types and efficiency of fuels utilized and the ultimate performance.

Energy Sources

The actual source of energy used by the muscles in running or any other kind of activity is ATP (Adenosine Tri Phosphate). It can be generated either aerobically or anaerobically (with or without oxygen). All running events use a combination of the two systems. Distance running, which we will define here as any event over 2 miles, primarily uses aerobic metabolism; but cannot work without the contributions from anaerobic metabolism.

Anaerobic energy sources are favored at the start of exercise and when the intensity of exercise is greater than can be supported by the available oxygen supply using aerobic sources. Anaerobic sources are used to varying degrees throughout the exercise session depending on the intensity and duration of the exercise.

There are two sources of energy in the anaerobic system, the phosphate system and the lactate system.

Phosphate System

The phosphate system consists of small stores of high energy ATP and Creatine Phosphate (CP) in the muscle. The phosphate system is the primary system used in events taking 10 to 20 seconds(short sprints). When the store is exhausted, additional energy must be generated to replenish the phosphate pool or keep the muscles working. The stores can be regenerated and used over and over again.

Lactate System

The lactate system utilizes glycogen (sugar) and glucose in the absence of oxygen. The glycogen is stored locally in the muscles and remotely in the liver and the glucose is present in the blood. This system is more correctly referred to as oxygen independent glycolysis. The higher the energy requirement the more the local stores in the muscle are favored. The glucose and glycogen form both ATP and pyruvate. In the absence of oxygen, the pyruvate is converted to lactate and hydrogen ions. Lactate is often thought of as a "waste product". In the presence of oxygen, however, it can be easily converted back to pyruvate to become a fuel used by muscles and the liver in the aerobic system.

Lactate is moved back and forth to other muscle groups and the liver via the bloodstream to provide fuel in needed areas. This process is known as the "lactate shuttle".

When the rate of production exceeds the rate of removal, the lactate and other waste products begin to accumulate, bloodstream pH level, (acidity), rises and the muscles do not function as well and begin to "burn". An example of the result of lactate accumulation is the "tying up" of the 800 meter runner the last 100 yards after starting too fast. Examples most of us have felt are the burning from too many sit ups, (lactate in the abdominal muscles), or the quadriceps burning felt when bicycling or running up a steep hill. At increasing intensities, lactate levels increase limiting the duration of performance. One of the goals of training is to have the muscles alter both lactate production and consumption thus lowering the lactate levels and allowing increased performance and/or duration. This can be optimized by specific training.

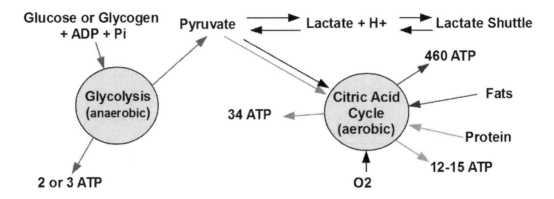

Lactate and the hydrogen ion accumulation is limited if the intensity of the exercise is low enough for pyruvate to be utilized in the aerobic system to make more ATP.

Aerobic System
At lower exercise intensities, energy conversion is primarily aerobic. The availability of oxygen allows multiple aerobic energy sources to be added to anaerobic glycolysis. The energy for aerobic metabolism comes from two main sources: glycogen (muscle and liver glycogen, blood glucose) and fat. Fat is stored in muscle as well as other major stores.

Glycogen is the most readily available source of aerobic energy and the primary energy source up to about 30 minutes of exercise. With oxygen availability, glycogen becomes pyruvate to be used aerobically. Aerobic glycolysis is capable of providing more than 10 times the energy of anaerobic glycolysis but at a slower rate since oxygen is required.

After 30 minutes, fat is mobilized from fat stores and becomes a major contributor. Fat can contribute tremendous energy, (more than 10 times glycogen), but at an increasingly slower rate because of increased oxygen demand.

There is always a combination of glycogen and fat usage with the relative contributions at any time determined by the intensity and duration of exercise and the state of training of the individual. More intense exercise will tend to burn more of the most readily available fuels, (eg muscle glycogen). As intensity is lowered liver and blood glycogen are utilized more. As the intensity of the exercise decreases more, a higher ratio of fat is used. At paces about 30% slower than your 10K race pace (1.3 x 10K pace/mile), or 20% slower than marathon race pace you should be utilizing the highest amount of fat for fuel per minute.

As the duration of the exercise extends, a continuing higher percentage of fat is utilized. From 30 - 60 % of marathon energy can be provided by fat.

Oxidation Energy Sources

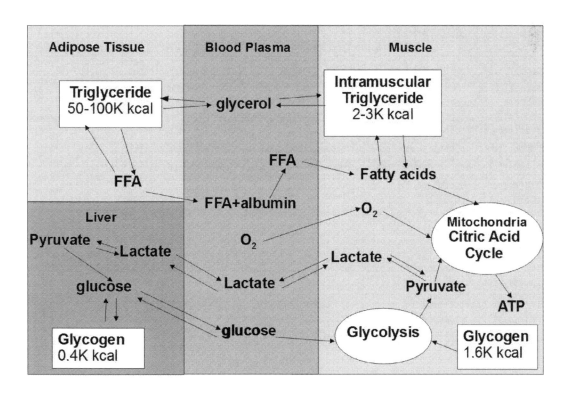

There is a finite storage of glycogen which can be increased somewhat through training. However, even in the best of circumstances, these stores will run out usually after 1 hour 45 minutes to 2 hours of hard running. Running longer distances would not be possible without the ability to use fat as a simultaneous fuel source. There are nearly unlimited supplies of fat. One pound of fat contains enough energy to run over 50 kilometers (31.2 mi). Fat, however, cannot be easily metabolized without the presence of muscle glycogen and the pyruvate which powers the aerobic system. Therefore if muscle glycogen levels are badly depleted, fat is available but cannot be utilized leading to a drastic drop in performance ("hitting the wall"). This is why it is important not to start too fast in long training runs or races and "waste" your muscle glycogen stores. It is possible through proper training to increase the contribution of fat to the overall energy production by more than 20 %; thereby sparing muscle glycogen and extending the time until its depletion.

At lower intensities more glycogen from the liver and bloodstream can be utilized. This spares some of the important muscle glycogen stores so that efficient aerobic metabolism using fat can be maintained for a longer duration. In marathon and ultramarathon events, liver glycogen depletion has been observed indicating that ingestion of sugar or sugared drinks may be necessary during the event.

In exercise lasting over 4 hours, protein may be broken down, first from muscle enzymes and then from the liver and muscle tissue itself, to make the necessary glycogen for fuel. This method of energy conversion is extremely inefficient and the body's last resort for survival. Studies have shown that protein may contribute 5 to 10% of marathon energy.

Running the marathon requires a combination of both carbohydrate and fat metabolism. The physiologic goals of a marathon training program are to provide enough endurance training to optimize aerobic metabolism. This results in the ability to metabolize higher percentages of fat, to facilitate increased storage of carbohydrates, to increase lactate consumption and decrease its production resulting in the ability to run faster paces aerobically.

Muscles

Proper marathon training will produce adaptations that allow greater consumption and utilization of energy. Some of these changes occur at the local muscle level and include better utilization of oxygen through increased size and number of mitochondria (little energy factories within the cells) and an increase in their aerobic enzymes. These muscles can more easily mobilize and use fat for energy, which helps to preserve the carbohydrate stores. The body also develops a greater ability to store and utilize carbohydrates. Some muscle fibers can be adapted for aerobic or anaerobic metabolism exercise. For the marathon, you want to adapt these convertible muscles for aerobic or endurance work. Through training there will be an increase in the number of capillaries for better nutrient supply as well as an increase in the amount of muscle tissue.

The ability to perform work with our muscles is dependent on our muscular composition and our muscular fitness level. There are two major types of skeletal muscles: slow red and fast contracting. Slow red muscle, because it has lots of blood vessels to carry the nutrients, lots of myoglobin to transport oxygen and lots of mitochondria, consumes oxygen well and generates ATP or energy with aerobic metabolism. Because of its aerobic ability and its resistance to fatigue, this is the primary muscle type of the long distance runner. Slow red muscles tend to be long and thin, note the slender legs of most marathoners. Slow refers to its ability to be slow to fatigue.

Fast contracting muscle may be either white or red. White uses the anaerobic phosphate or lactate energy systems. Red has the same characteristics as the slow red, but can use either anaerobic or aerobic metabolism to perform work. Note that fast white muscles usually are those that can hypertrophy or get big and are the primary muscles of body builders, sprinters and jumpers. People with a high percentage of fast white muscle fibers may not perform well in endurance events. With a couple of exceptions which are mentioned below, it has been thought that we are born with a muscle make up consisting of a fixed ratio of both kinds of fibers and cannot change it. The most notable exception is that fast red muscle may be converted to use either aerobic or anaerobic metabolism through appropriate training. Some studies have shown that ultradistance runners who have broken down huge amounts of muscle tissue during strenuous events rebuild with slow red fibers. This would be considered a rather extreme way to alter muscle makeup, however. An easier way to convert those fast red muscles is by endurance training, (increasing mileage). Studies of highly trained individuals have shown no difference in the mitochrondrial aerobic enzymes levels between the slow red and the fast red muscle fibers indicating that their endurance characteristics are equivalent. The fast red fibers may be activated by either faster aerobic running, (eg 15k to marathon race pace), or longer slow running, (running over 2 hours at the proper slow training pace).

The body's energy system design is beautifully efficient. The highest energy, shortest term fuels are stored closest to the point where the work is done in the muscle cells. Bulkier long term fuels used in endurance activities are stored at more remote places in the body (e.g. liver glycogen, fat in stores). These remote sources are delivered to the muscle cells along with oxygen from the lungs by the cardiovascular system, which is also responsible for removing waste products. The final stage of this process is at the cellular level where enzyme and other biochemical processes are adapted to efficiently convert various fuels to ATP. This cellular adaptation is one of the most trainable aspects of the human body, and is responsible for much of the training response having to do with endurance.

Adaptations of the cardiovascular and respiratory systems are also important results of training. The heart muscle increases in size, weight and the amount of blood it can pump. Resting and submaximal exercise heart rates are decreased. The amount of blood that the heart pumps, called the stroke volume, increases resulting in a greater amount of oxygen extracted through better distribution of blood to the working muscles. As more blood goes through the muscles, it carries more oxygen resulting in increased performance.

VO2 max

One of the most important training adaptations is an increase in the maximal oxygen uptake, called VO2 Max, which is a quantitative measure of a person's capacity for aerobic energy transfer (the ability to do work). An improvement in VO2 Max thus increases the amount of work you can do, that is you can run faster and/or farther. Variables that determine VO2 Max are heredity, sex, body composition (the amount of lean body tissue), age and training. Obviously you can do nothing about several of these variables, but improvements of 20-30% in maximal oxygen uptake because of training have been observed. VO2 max peaks within 6 months to 2 years after starting an endurance training program. However, even after it has leveled off, it is still possible to improve performance. Typical marathoners are able to maintain their pace using approximately 75-80% of VO2 Max for the well over 2 hours required. Higher mileage athletes are able to work for prolonged periods at higher levels of VO2 Max. The ability to run at higher percentages of VO2 Max may be explained changes in the lactate system, more enzymes, more mitochondria and increased efficiency. The increasing intensity of exercise can cause lactate to accumulate and impair performance. Improving the lactate system means that you can run harder for a longer period of time and use the lactate as an additional energy source. Studies have shown that lactate production and consumption can be easily shifted by endurance training. The response to increased mileage is lowered production and increased consumption allowing the body to run faster aerobically.

Endurance

Although changes in VO2 max due to training are limited to perhaps 30%, much larger changes in endurance (the ability to maintain a submaximal work effort for long durations) can be obtained through training. This is apparently because endurance activities utilize aerobic energy delivery systems that can be greatly enhanced by specific training. Much of this is due to increases in the number and quality of mitochondria in the muscles with continued training. Changes in endurance achievable by training are probably in the range of 100 to 1 or 10,000%!

Understanding that maximal performance levels (VO2 max and top speed) are not as important as endurance in achieving performance in a marathon is critical for training. How fast you are makes no difference if you cannot maintain the pace for 26 miles 385 yards.

Efficiency

Neuromuscular coordination refers to the ability of athletes to perform their sports in a smooth, balanced and fluid motion. For running, this ability is known as efficiency or economy. It has been suggested that marathoners are more efficient than middle distance runners. This may be because marathon training induces greater changes in efficiency than training for shorter distances. It may be because more efficient runners tend to be more successful in marathons.

Muscles move in groups rather than individually. Some muscles must be contracted (agonistic) and coordinated with each other to produce the maximum contractile force. The antagonist muscles must relax in coordination with the contraction so that they don't provide unwanted resistance to the movement. Other muscles in the body also must coordinate in both contraction and relaxation to stabilize the body and maintain other body actions. During endurance activities, in each muscle, groups of muscle fibers are used to perform work while others are rested and vice versa. These complex processes are governed by neuromuscular coordination.

Neuromuscular coordination causes each movement to occur in the correct sequence and timing with just the right amount of force. Skilled performance occurs when the nerve impulses reach the proper muscle at the correct time to create the movement pattern. One of the important aspects of neuromuscular facilitation is the concept of reciprocal inhibition. When nerve impulses are sent to the muscles to contract, inhibitory impulses are carried to the antagonistic muscles to relax so that they do not interfere with the speed and forces of the desired movement. Controlled movements with less than maximum force and speed need some voluntary resistance. One of the determiners of skill has been shown to be excessive contraction by those antagonistic muscles.

The skilled athlete recruits a coordinated movement pattern without having to think about it. For the marathoner, this means being able to run at marathon pace throughout the marathon. The method of gaining the skill is specific repetitious practice until the recruitment of movement pattern changes from conscious control to conditioned reflex. The more skilled we are at specific running movements, the less energy we will expend and the more efficient we are. Because the adaptation is quite specific, pace training (some training at race pace) has been shown to be effective in improving efficiency. For marathoning, some running at marathon pace is appropriate and necessary for good performance.

Central Governor or Anticipatory Regulation

Exercise scientists have long argued about which system is responsible for exhaustion and why/how runners can speed up when the finish is in sight in spite of supposed spent fuel, muscle and other types of fatigue. In fact, depletion, body heat and other fatigue models have failed to totally explain exhaustion.

The current proposed concept has been termed by some as the central governor where the afferent nervous system inputs to the brain are used to govern or regulate performance. The concept of anticipatory regulation is that the afferent inputs including both physiological and psychological data let the brain regulate output to sustain performance for the exercise. The main source of regulation is change in pace in response to usage of glycogen, generation of heat, production and consumption of metabolites such lactate and other variables. The brain can integrate all of the body systems using a known endpoint to maintain and sustain the exercise at a level to avoid collapse before the finish.

Central Governor theory seems to support a strong argument for specificity of training since the brain would have to learn how to sense and maintain proper levels for completion for a given event.

Keys to Success

One important measure of a successful training program in any sport is economy, "getting the most bang for your buck". Economy has two benefits: 1) you can achieve a higher level of training with the same outlay of effort and 2) the risk of injury is minimized or reduced. A successful training program employs all of the following:

- Hard/Easy Cycles
- Progressive Overload
- Specificity
- Injury Prevention Techniques

Hard/Easy Cycles and Progressive Overload

Training is accomplished by the adaptation to repeated stress. If overload or stress is repeated many times, it results in specific adaptation of the body strengthening resistance to that stress. In running, stress can be applied by increased speed and/or distance. Adaptation does not take place during the overload or stress period, but during the recovery or rest periods between stresses. During stress microscopic cell destruction takes place and working muscles and cells are depleted of necessary enzymes and nutrients. During recovery periods, microscopic rebuilding takes place along with some overcompensation. This overcompensation is what is referred to as "training effect". It allows you to slowly increase the overload over time to build strength or endurance, a process known as "progressive overload". Over time, provided the body rebuilds as fast or faster than the progressive overload, the body will adapt to increasing stress level.

In a runner's training program, overload (hard workouts) can be achieved through either added speed or distance, while recovery takes place only when both speed and distance are minimized (easy workouts). To quantify these, the following definitions are given:

HARD: a workout in which the distance is greater than 20 percent of a runner's weekly mileage or a workout run at greater than 85% of the maximum pace the runner could run for that training distance.

EASY: a workout in which the distance is less than 10 per cent of a runner's weekly mileage and is run at 80% or less of the maximum pace the runner could run for that training distance.

The more often you can overload and recover, the better. The key limitation is recovery. If the overload is too great, it may take so long to recover that you don't get the maximum number of overload/recovery cycles and you may get injured. If the recovery is inadequate, you will not have the strengthened resources to overload during the next cycle. This leads to injury.

Adequate recovery between overload cycles requires 48 hours or longer. Forty-eight hours is the minimum time needed to replenish enzymes and nutrients, such as glycogen, within the muscle cells after a hard workout. For this reason, most successful training programs have at least one easy workout day following each hard workout day to allow for recovery. An easy workout, in lieu of total rest, can actually help speed the recovery by increasing circulation to the recovering tissue which helps flush out wastes.

Specificity

Adaptation to overload tends to respond to the specific stress involved. Therefore, the stress should overload the muscles and other systems used in the activity for which you are training and the stress should simulate the type of activity (i.e. aerobic, anaerobic, etc.) An economical training program should be tailored to the type of activity for which you are training (i.e. endurance running requires long duration runs for training as opposed to short sprints). A corollary to specificity is that the component parts of a sport can be trained for separately and specifically. This will be discussed later.

Injury Prevention Techniques

Any training is better than no training. Hence, the most important aspect of any training program is injury prevention. Useful strategies and tactics for doing this are:

- Having a training plan.
- Separating speed and distance.
- Allowing adequate recovery between hard workouts.
- Monitoring the response of your body to training.
- Proactive injury treatment
- Utilizing coaches and clinics.

Training Plans

The best strategy is to devise and write down a training plan which has target times and distances which will stress, but not break the runner, and will allow adequate recovery between hard workouts. Long term training increases, (e.g. building mileage), should be gradual, at a rate of 5-10% per week or less.

Once a training plan is established, it should be viewed as a flexible framework around and within which the runner can employ various tactics to lessen the risk of injury. These can include variations in terrain, surface and shoes. If necessary, individual workouts can be eliminated or changed or the overall plan can be modified.

Separating Speed and Distance

A key technique used in training is functionally specific workouts. These workouts concentrate on one element of the training at a time, independent of the other components being trained. This independent training is highly effective and allows one part of the body to rest while the other is trained, minimizing overuse injuries.

Specific elements of long distance running are speed, (aerobic power), and distance (endurance). These can be trained using workout combinations shown in the speed/distance matrix below.

Workout Effort

		DISTANCE	
	<10%	20%	30%
		Weekly Mileage	

SPEED		<10%	20%	30%
	80%	Easy	Long	Very Long
	90%	Hard		
	100%	Very Hard		

The filled in squares in the matrix effectively separate hard or very hard efforts in either speed or distance from their counterparts on the other axis and are recommended training techniques. A complete training program includes workouts that are speed specific and those that are distance specific.

Combinations of speed and distance, (blank squares in matrix), may be effective training techniques, but provide a much higher risk of injury because the total stress is higher.

For long distance runs, such as the marathon, 95% of all training should be specific to endurance. Hence, nearly all hard workouts should be either long or very long distance runs done at an easy speed. Speed training is used most effectively only during the final weeks before the event for sharpening or for periodic fitness measurement.

Recovery
In order to get the training benefit of hard workouts, there must be adequate recovery provided to let the body rebuild before another hard workout. Otherwise, instead of the desired positive training effect, the result will be cumulative damage and, ultimately, injury The matrix below gives the number of recovery, (easy workout), days which are recommended following various workout efforts. Typical workout weeks employ 3 hard workouts alternated with 4 recovery days.

Recovery Days After Workouts

	DISTANCE Weekly Mileage		
SPEED	<10%	20%	30%
80%	0	1	2
90%	1	3	5
100%	2	5	8+

Note that we have included recommended recovery days for mixed speed and distance workouts. This can be used as a guide for those of you who overdo occasionally or run races (100% speed).

Self Monitoring

A very useful aid is a training diary where you can record your training plans and goals. You can note resting heart rate (HR), training HR, recovery HR, weight, daily and weekly mileage, times plus a general comment on how you feel each day. An example is shown in the Appendix. Learning how your body reacts to overload and when to rest is important in maintaining health. You can use monitored heart rates to measure the result of effort of running and recovery. Heart Rate recovery consists of two phases, short and long term. During the short term phase, the HR drops rapidly from the exercise rate to about 20 to 30 beats/minute above the resting HR. The long term phase may last for varying periods depending on the total stress of the run. Monitoring how long it takes for your HR to return to the resting rate is a good way to see whether a run has been too hard and a rest day is in order. Usually this long term period should be several hours, but it may last up to 24 hours after a long run. The guidelines for recovery time and HR are different for each individual. A diary can help you determine your particular normals and monitor yourself.

It is important to dispel the old myth "No pain, no gain". It is possible to train and improve by hard work that does not include pain. It is not possible to train at all if you are sick or injured. A good training program works to prevent these complications. Dick Brown, the former coach of Athletics West, felt that a major part of his role was to keep his athletes healthy. There is no one "right" way to train and each runner needs to learn how his or her body reacts to different overloads and what works best. But remember, overtraining does not help anyone and a rest day is definitely in order when there is:

- An increase in resting HR of 5 beats per minute or more
- A sudden weight loss of 5 or more pounds
- A feeling of excessive thirst
- A sluggish or very tired feeling
- The start of illness such as sore throat or cough
- Difficulty sleeping

Some of the questions most commonly asked by runners involved in a training program are of the form "What happens if

- I miss a day because of illness or injury?
- I need a rest day and my schedule calls for a hard day?
- I miss a whole week of training?
- My ... hurts, should I run on it?

The answer to all of these questions is "Learn to listen to your body and respond to its needs!". If something is painful while you are running on it, that is your body's way of telling you that it is being abused. Heed its cry. Skipping a day or a week will not cause you to fall into immediate decay. Do not feel guilty, do not be compulsive, and do not add the missed workouts or mileage into your future schedule. If your body tells you it needs a rest, listen. The major goal is to remain healthy, injury free and enjoy your running, not to rack up as many miles and consecutive days as you can. If you have missed workouts, it may be necessary to drop back to an easier schedule for several days or weeks and then gradually return to the previous one. Remember, only you can hear your body protest, and only you can do something about it.

Proactive Injury Treatment

By most estimates, 50 - 70% of all runners will experience an injury annually that will cause them to take time off from their sport. Fortunately, running does not produce the traumatic kinds of injuries that might be experienced in sports such as sky diving or downhill ski racing. The preponderance of running injuries is, in fact, chronic soft tissue inflammations. The onset of these injuries is not sudden, but usually follows a history of neglect and abuse. Running injuries are caused; they don't "just happen".

This class of soft tissue degenerations or inflammations are often referred to as "overuse" injuries, a term which may be misleading they are more often a result of changes in training rather than simple volume of training. Because of their nature, three fourths of running injuries could probably be avoided or reduced with early detection and treatment.

There are four stages exhibited by running injuries:

Stage 1
Symptoms: Pain noticed only after running, sometimes hours after or the next morning.
Prognosis: 1-2 day recovery possible with proper treatment and elimination of the cause.
Treatment: Ice, Compression, Elevation and Massage

Stage 2
Symptoms: "Discomfort" or "tightness", but not pain felt while running. Normal running and racing still possible.
Prognosis: 4 - 7 day recovery possible with proper treatment and elimination of the cause.
Treatment: 4 day rest or a non-exacerbating alternate activity, Ice Compression, Elevation and Massage. Seek professional help if no improvement or worse after 7 days rest and treatment.

Stage 3
Symptoms: More severe discomfort described as "pain" felt while running. Runner feels compelled to reduce training and/or racing levels.
Prognosis: 2 to 4 week recovery possible with proper treatment and elimination of the cause.
Treatment: 4 - 7day rest or a non-exacerbating alternate activity, Ice Compression, Elevation, and Massage. Seek professional help if no improvement or worse after 7 days rest and treatment. Requires rehabilitation with a return to running when no pain on activity.

Stage 4
Symptoms: Severe pain. Runner cannot run.
Prognosis: 6 week or longer recovery possible with proper treatment and elimination of the cause.
Treatment: Seek professional help immediately. Requires professional treatment and rehabilitation. Return to running only when no pain with activity.

Injuries do not develop through these four levels overnight. This is why most of them can be dealt with before they affect performance. The key is detection at stage 1 or 2 and aggressive treatment before further progression. Unfortunately, this is not often done. The usual scenario of progressive injury is: "Gee, my foot, leg, etc is sore. Couldn't have been the running I did this morning. Hmmm, when I'm running it feels kind of tight where it was sore yesterday. Wow, that was tight yesterday, maybe I'll run fewer miles tomorrow. Well, it's still sore. I'll go run on it to see if it still hurts. Ouch! Better not run on this, it might cause permanent damage. "

Rather than denial or fear of the loss of fitness, the runner needs to adopt a proactive posture that assumes a potential injury and treats it in an early stage. This aggressive preventative early treatment behavior should be considered part of the sport of running; not the " wait till it's broken to fix it" behavior that most runners do.

Steps to proactive injury prevention and treatment:

Expect to get injured. If you are aware, you will be able to detect injuries in the making.

Keep a first aid kit. You should have several paper cups with water frozen in them for ice massage, ice cubes and zip lock bags for ice packs and an elastic bandage for wrapping the ice packs against the injury. To avoid frostbite or nerve damage, use only water ice for cold packs and limit exposure to 10-15 minutes.

"Nuke" injuries in the making. Immediately ice after running any spot that "feels" funny. Ice massage with paper cup popsicles or wrap with an ice bag for 10-15 minutes then allow area to warm. Repeat several times a day if possible until there are no more symptoms. Rest the injury a day or two.

Admit that getting well is more important than training. Keep injuries from progressing beyond level 1 or level 2. At those levels, a little rest and treatment can prevent lots of time off later.

Admit that injuries are caused. They are not an "act of God". If you want a long term fix for your problem, you must identify and treat the cause, not just the symptoms.

Don't be afraid to seek professional advice. Some doctors are familiar with athletes' needs and can help you get back to the sport quickly. If your doctor is not interested in seeking the cause and returning you to running as soon as possible, get another doctor, preferably one who runs.

Anti-Inflammatories

While anti-inflammatories may reduce pain, there is a mounting body of evidence that they interfere with the bodies normal healing processes. They, along with other pain killers should be avoided if possible and not used to continue training.

Coaching and Clinics

In most cases, runners benefit from outside coaching. A good coach will have an unbiased view of cause/effect relationships and may be more likely to protect the runner from injury than the runner himself. Many running clubs have coaching available or can provide you with group training sessions and clinics where support and answers to your questions are available. The Road Runners Club of America has a certification program for road running coaches. You can look for certified coaches in your area by visiting their website at http://www.rrca.org/

Returning to Running After Injury

You can return to running only when you can walk without pain. To start, go to a local track where you can quit if you have pain. Walk 2 laps (1/2 mile), then stretch lightly. Jog or slowly run the straights of the track and walk the curves for 4 – 8 laps. Make certain you stop and go home if you have any discomfort. Finish the workout by walking 2 laps, then stretching and icing the previously injured area. It will take about as long to return to your training schedule as you were off running. Assuming you did the track run with no pain, rest the next day and start to resume your training schedule. The first week, run every other day, the easy (short) distance and half of the long run distance. The second week, again run every other day but do the longer midweek distances and ¾ of the long run distance. Stop at any time if you have pain and resume treatment. Never try to return to running by starting at the long run distance. Do at least 2-3 shorter runs before attempting to do even half of the long run.

Base Building

Plans, Paces and Progressions

There are three phases to marathon training. The first phase is base building during which the runner builds the strength and endurance base necessary for specific marathon training. This phase may take 4 to 6 months for the beginning marathoner. The second phase is the sharpening phase, which employs specific marathon workouts to achieve maximum marathon performance. This phase is usually 8 to 10 weeks. The last phase is the race preparation phase that encompasses final preparation, planning and resting during the week or so before the race. Twenty six week marathon training programs for novice, beginning, recreational, intermediate and advanced marathoners are listed throughout the book to be used as examples. Although the mileages may seem daunting to the new marathon trainee, they are easily achievable using the conservative progressions listed in the book and running at the proper easy paces.

Some Definitions

The specific endurance training requirements for a marathon are too demanding to be "done from scratch". The average runner who runs 20 to 30 miles per week would quickly break down if he attempted to do 20 mile marathon training runs because of the lack of an adequate base. To run long training runs, you must run enough miles to adequately adapt your body to the stresses involved.

What is adequate mileage base for a marathon? It depends on your goal and your body. If you are a beginner and your goal is to finish, you may do so on 40 to 45 miles per week if that training is very specific for the marathon. For experienced runners who want to achieve a good performance, we recommend a minimum of 60-65 miles per week. With a 65 mile a week base, you would easily be able to tolerate the 20 mile training runs and some specific "speed work" during the sharpening phase. Part of your training involves becoming attuned to your body and being able to judge how many miles your body will tolerate; how it will respond to the different training techniques and what is optimal for you.

Before going any further, we will reiterate some training terms in the context of building a mileage base. Later, as we get into the sharpening phase we will expand these definitions.

EASY: a description of effort and can be used to describe the runs where rest and rebuilding occurs. Easy can either refer to pace or distance. "Easy" is a pace that is about 80% or less of the pace that the distance could be run in a race and a distance of 10% or less of the weekly mileage. Many runners do not realize the importance of easy runs and do not get adequate rest. The consequence of this is that they cannot get the benefits of hard runs because they are too fatigued. The body does not have a chance to rebuild in response to overload in such situations. Charts of "easy" training paces (80% or less effort) are given in the Appendix.

HARD: also a description of effort and describes training when the principle of overload applies. Hard can also be defined in terms of distance or pace. During the base building phase, it refers to runs of longer mileage (more than 20% of the total weekly mileage) that are run at an "easy" pace (80% or less effort). In the sharpening phase, hard workouts will use increased intensity or pace.

Building Endurance
The basic training for all distance racing is endurance training. The runner must have the stamina to cover the desired distance. Cardiovascular endurance comes first. Then the specific muscles become stronger, followed by the connective tissues, tendons and ligaments. Injury often occurs because the runner wrongly feels that he has the stamina to run the required number of miles, but actually lacks the muscular and connective tissue strength, which develops much more slowly. Base building for the marathon should follow a schedule designed to build mileage slowly and comfortably to the level where your body can tolerate the necessary long training runs.

During the base building phase, a general scheme of workouts over a 7 day (weekly) period might look something like this:

Day	1	2	3	4	5	6	7
Normalized Distance	3	1	1	2	1	2	1

The normalized distances are based on the hard runs being either 2 or 3 times the distance of the easy runs. All of the runs are done at any easy (80% or less) effort. This results in maximum improvements in aerobic metabolism, which lead to, increased aerobic enzyme production, better fat utilization and adaptation of convertible muscle to aerobic use. There are three "hard" days per week and 4 easy recovery days. One of the hard runs is particularly long and is followed by two recovery days. Most runners refer to this workout as their "long run" of the week. It is the basis for their endurance training. The ultimate goal of the base building phase is to slowly build up the length of your daily runs to the point where the long run simulates the endurance requirements of the marathon.

Beginning

Many runners will start marathon training from schedules that are low in total miles, run at too high a pace, do not reflect a hard/easy structure and do not support 7 days a week of running. The first improvement to be made is to slow them down and adopt the hard/easy approach to training. The easy days may in fact be days of no running at all or may mean playing golf or bicycling. But you must have hard days for overload and easy days for recovery to get maximum benefit from training.

More advanced runners with higher weekly mileage should also examine their weekly workouts to see if hard/easy cycles are being used. They may already be running a total mileage consistent with marathon training (6-7 miles/day), but not be completing long runs sufficient for proper marathon training requirements (20 miles or more). Base building in this group may not require running more miles per week as much as it may require slowly changing workouts to adapt to longer runs.

Pace

During the base building phase, the primary goal is to develop endurance. Hence the emphasis for the hard runs should be on increased distance rather than speed (remember the matrix). Training at 80% or less of the pace you could run in a race of the same distance is an adequate speed to accomplish this. Most runners will find this slower than they have been training. This is an advantage because it allows them to run further in training. Pace charts are in the Appendix to help you decide how slowly you should be running. Other ways to tell if you are running at the proper pace are by perceived exertion and the "talk test". If you feel that you are working hard or that the pace will be difficult to maintain, slow down until the work level is easy or moderate. If you cannot carry on a conversation with another runner or need to speak between gasps of air, slow down to what would be a conversational level. You can also monitor effort using training heart rates. The exercise heart rate is based on a calculated percent of maximum HR. A rough estimate of your easy training heart rate can be computed by subtracting your age from 185. During easy training runs your heart rate should be lower than this number. A complete set of training heart rates is included in the Appendix.

If you are increasing your mileage a great deal, you are getting all the stress or overload needed without doing any fast paced running. Be patient and stay healthy, speed will be developed later when your body has the strength to handle its increased demands.

Mileage Progressions

Once you have established a hard/easy routine in your training, you can begin to add mileage to build a base for the marathon. Mileage increases should be no more than 5% per week. A hard/easy version of progression is to add 10% every two weeks. To increase mileage, first increase the length of your longer runs. Increase the length of your rest runs only when they are well below 10% of your weekly mileage. This will assure that you get maximum recovery. Plan your schedule to allow you to reach long runs of about 20 miles 8 to 10 weeks prior to the marathon. How long does the long run need to be for marathon performance? For the beginning marathoner, you need to run for about the same length of time as you will run during the marathon. This means about a 20 mile run, if you run it at the recommended 80% easy effort. The balance of your training may not support runs longer than this. Attempts at longer distances may lead to injury or extreme fatigue. For those with more experience, especially those trying to improve performance, a few runs up to and possibly beyond the marathon distance could be valuable. Try to keep your schedule close to the 3:1:1:2:1:2:1 daily ratios discussed above.

Each workout should consist of at least a 5 minute warm-up, (a fast walk or slow jog), before the run and a five minute cool-down, (again a slow jog or walk), after the run. These can be incorporated into the training run by simply starting and finishing at a slower pace. Increased mileage makes a stretching program a necessity, especially for the muscles in the lower back and the entire back of the legs. A program of slow stretching should be done after the completion of the workout at least 3 times per week; stretching every day is recommended and more beneficial. A specific stretching program is described in the Supplemental Training Chapter. Some runners like to break up their longer mileage workout days into two runs. Endurance training benefits still are derived from this due to incomplete recovery between runs. However, the benefits are certainly not as great as from a single longer run. Specificity demands running 20+ mile runs if you want to train adequately for the marathon.

To assist you to devise a personal training program, five base building mileage progressions are given below. Remember to use the training pace and heart rate charts given in the appendix to determine a target effort for your training runs.

Training Fatigue
During the base building phase, it is normal to feel some fatigue. The fatigue may be most apparent as runners reach long run distances of 15 miles or more. This is the point where runners' bodies are adapting to enlisting new energy sources.

Novice Marathon Basebuilding

Starting Point
Three months of running experience and a base of 8-12 miles per week.

NOTE: This is a "minimalist" program designed for an active person with good general fitness but limited running experience. For best results we recommend a better starting base and the Beginner program.

Goals
Long term: To finish a marathon. Medium term: To build a base that will support some 20 mile training runs and some minimal marathon specific speedwork during the sharpening phase (weeks 18-25).

Mileage Progression

Week	S	M	T	W	T	F	S	Total
1	4	0	2W	2	2W	2	0	12
2	5	0	2W	3	2W	2	0	14
3	6	0	2W	3	2W	3	0	16
4	7	0	2W	4	2W	3	0	18
5	8	0	2W	4	2W	4	0	20
6	9	0	2W	4	2	4	0	21
7	10	0	2	4	2	4	0	22
8	10	0	2	5	2	4	0	23
9	10	0	2	5	2	5	0	24
10	12	0	2	5	2	5	0	26
11	12	0	2	6	2	6	0	28
12	13	0	3	6	2	6	0	30
13	14	0	3	6	3	6	0	32
14	15	0	3	7	3	6	0	34
15	16	0	3	7	3	7	0	36
16	16	0	3	8	3	8	0	38
17	18	0	3	8	3	8	0	40

(W) Walk the distance listed, the walk increases endurance while reducing the injury risk.

All runs done at an easy, (80% effort), training pace. See pace/heart rate charts in Appendix.

Beginning Marathon Basebuilding

Starting Point
Six months of running experience and a base of 20 miles per week

Goals
Long term: To finish a marathon. Medium term: To build a base that will support some 20 mile training runs and some marathon specific speedwork during the sharpening phase (weeks 18-25).

Mileage Progression

Week	S	M	T	W	T	F	S	Total
1	6	0	2	4	2	4	0	18
2	7	0	2	4	2	4	0	19
3	8	0	2	4	2	4	0	20
4	9	0	2	4	2	4	0	21
5	10	0	2	4	2	4	0	22
6	10	0	2	5	2	4	0	23
7	10	0	2	5	2	5	0	24
8	12	0	2	5	2	5	0	26
9	12	0	2	6	2	6	0	28
10	13	0	3	6	2	6	0	30
11	14	0	3	6	3	6	0	32
12	15	0	3	7	3	6	0	34
13	16	0	3	7	3	7	0	36
14	16	0	3	8	3	8	0	38
15	18	0	3	8	3	8	0	40
16	16	0	4	8	4	8	0	40
17	20	0	4	8	4	8	0	44

All runs done at an easy, (80% effort), training pace. See pace/heart rate charts in Appendix.

Recreational Marathon Basebuilding

Starting Point
Experienced runner, may have run one or more marathons; has a base of 25 to 30 miles per week

Goals
Long term: to improve marathon time by building better endurance and using more specific training. Medium term: to achieve an endurance base, which will support 20 mile runs and some marathon specific speedwork during the sharpening phase (weeks 18-25).

Mileage Progression

Week	S	M	T	W	T	F	S	Total
1	8	0	3	6	3	6	0	26
2	9	0	3	6	3	6	0	27
3	10	0	3	6	3	6	0	28
4	10	0	3	7	3	6	0	29
5	10	0	3	7	3	7	0	30
6	12	0	3	7	3	7	0	32
7	12	0	4	8	3	7	0	34
8	13	0	4	8	3	8	0	36
9	14	0	4	8	4	8	0	38
10	15	0	4	9	4	8	0	40
11	16	0	4	9	4	9	0	42
12	16	0	5	10	4	9	0	44
13	17	0	5	10	4	10	0	46
14	18	0	5	10F	4	10	0	47
15	18	0	5	10F	5	10	0	48
16	19	0	5	10F	5	10	0	49
17	20	0	5	10F	5	10	0	50

 (F) Fartlek runs include strength building sessions which consist of running 1 minute hard followed by 4 minutes easy for the middle 5 miles. Otherwise all runs are done at an easy, (80% effort), training pace. See pace/heart rate charts in Appendix.

Intermediate Marathon Basebuilding

Starting Point
Experienced runner, may have run one or more marathons; has a base of 35 to 40 miles per week

Goals
Long term: to improve marathon time by building better endurance and using more specific training. Medium term: to achieve an endurance base, which will support 20 mile runs and some marathon specific speedwork during the sharpening phase (weeks 18-25).

Mileage Progression

Week	S	M	T	W	T	F	S	Total
1	9	0	4	8	4	8	4	37
2	10	0	4	8	4	8	4	38
3	11	0	4	8	4	8	4	39
4	12	0	4	9	4	8	4	41
5	13	0	4	9	4	9	4	43
6	14	0	4	9	4	9	4	44
7	14	0	5	10	4	9	4	46
8	15	0	5	10	4	10	4	48
9	15	0	5	10	5	10	4	49
10	16	0	5	10	5	10	5	51
11	16	0	5	11	5	10	5	52
12	17	0	5	11	5	11	5	54
13	17	0	5	12	5	12	5	56
14	18	0	6	12F	5	12	5	58
15	18	0	6	12F	6	12	6	60
16	19	0	6	12F	6	12	6	61
17	20	0	6	12F	6	12	6	62

(F) Fartlek runs include strength building sessions which consist of running 1 minute hard followed by 4 minutes easy for the middle 6 miles. Otherwise all runs are done at an easy, (80% effort), training pace. See pace/heart rate charts in Appendix.

Advanced Marathon Basebuilding

Starting Point
Experienced road racer, most likely with previous marathon experience; has a mileage base of 50 miles per week

Goals
Long term: to improve marathon time by building extra endurance and speed. Medium term: to achieve a base, which will support runs of marathon length and marathon specific speed work during the sharpening phase (weeks 18-25).

Mileage Progression

Week	S	M	T	W	T	F	S	Total
1	14	4	4	10	4	10	4	50
2	14	4	5	10	4	10	5	52
3	15	5	5	10	4	10	5	54
4	16	5	5	10	5	10	5	56
5	16	5	5	11	5	11	5	58
6	17	5	5	12	5	12	5	61
7	18	5	6	12	5	12	5	63
8	18	5	6	12	6	12	6	65
9	19	6	6	12	6	12	6	67
10	20	6	6	12	6	12	6	68
11	22	6	6	12	6	12	6	70
12	23	6	6	14	6	12	6	73
13	22	6	6	14F	6	12	6	72
14	24	6	6	14F	6	12	6	74
15	22	6	7	14F	7	14	6	76
16	24	6	7	14F	7	14	6	78
17	22	7	7	14F	7	14	7	78

(F) Fartlek runs include strength building sessions which consist of running 1 minute hard followed by 4 minutes easy for the middle 7 miles. Otherwise all runs are done at an easy, (80% effort), training pace. See pace/heart rate charts in Appendix.

Getting Out The Door

Sometimes the most difficult part of training, especially during the base building period, is getting out the door to go run. This is true even for experienced highly competitive athletes. Most of them have little motivational "tricks" that work for them. Some of these helps are listed below. Writing down a planned workout schedule is the first place to start. You have then made a date with yourself to complete a series of workouts. Filling out the training diary and being able to check off or fill in the appropriate space often works as a reward. Seeing all those completed workouts certainly encourages you to keep on being able to fill the pages.

Goal setting is an aid to planning the workout schedule and a key motivator. To achieve your goals, you must go out and train. Achieving a goal motivates you to set a new one. Tell your family and friends some of your goals and ask for their support to help you meet them. Doing so is a commitment to your goal.

Call or arrange with a friend to meet you to run. You will feel obligated not to disappoint them and you may actually enjoy running with someone. If this idea works for you, plan weekly training sessions with others such as attending group runs. You can even go to a race and run at training pace if being with others is important to you.

Try to create a habit. Set aside a specific time to run and let everyone know that this is your time to run. If you're really having a hard time and can't tell if you're physically or really only mentally tired, try the 5 minute test. Tell yourself that you only need to run for 5 minutes. If you still feel terrible at the end of 5 minutes, quit and enjoy a rest day. Usually, since you're already out there and feeling better, you'll decide to complete the workout.

Give yourself rewards; have a latte or a cookie after running; plan a family activity after completing the week's schedule with their help. Buy yourself some new shoes or shorts for meeting your goal mileage base. Use whatever rewards appeal to you. Including your friends and family in the rewards also encourages them to be supportive of you and your goals. As you run more, it becomes addictive and you feel deprived if you don't do it. Often the running becomes its own intrinsic reward. Use the "Premack Principle". This involves making an activity that is usually done contingent on an activity you want to do. If you usually read the newspaper when you get home, make reading the paper depend on going out for your run first.

Incorporate variety, run a different course, try new shoes, call a new friend to run with you. Try to incorporate your running into your lifestyle. Run to work, then you'll need to get home somehow - run. Try running as a means of transportation at other times. Interest your family and friends in running so that you can run together and so they can understand your need to train. Be creative and enjoy your running.

When it is difficult to get out the door because you are sick or injured, listen to your body. Workout schedules are guidelines not requirements. It is always OK to skip a workout or take an easy day if your body or your mind needs the rest. You can train effectively only if you are healthy, so do all you can to stay that way.

Sharpening

Maximizing Performance

The primary goal of marathon training is to build endurance. Inherent in this goal is the establishment of a sufficient mileage base. The mileage base is not an end in itself, but is the means for creating the stamina to support the real key to training - hard/easy cycles and in particular, the long run. As your base mileage and stamina build, you are able to do more work in your long runs and recover using longer easy runs. Without the base and the stamina, the long runs would provide a stress that you could not recover from, stopping you from doing the multiple overload/recovery cycles necessary for training.

Once an adequate base has been established, you can improve marathon performance through sharpening. Sharpening is an 8 to 10 week period during which very specific training is used and enough of it is applied for adaptation to occur. To do this training you must have built a base that will allow you to do vigorous marathon specific workouts without breaking down your body.

Sharpening Workouts
Sharpening workouts can be categorized as one of three types: Endurance, Pace or Strength. Beginning marathoners should concentrate on endurance while intermediate and advanced marathoners can benefit from pace and strength training.

Endurance
The key to the marathon is the long distance endurance run. During the sharpening phase, runners should do as many long runs as is practical, up to one per week. These runs should be done at an easy pace to encourage fat metabolism and must be long enough (approximately 20 miles), to fatigue the primary endurance muscle fibers and bring into play the convertible fibers that are not normally used. Aching upper leg muscles, especially outer quadriceps, at the conclusion of a long run are normal. This is a sure sign that you have run far enough to stress the convertible fibers.

Pace
The purpose of pace training is to attain maximum efficiency at race speeds and develop the ability to handle lactate consistent with race effort. Pace training for the marathon is achieved by running short distances at goal marathon race pace. An important side benefit is the development of pace judgment (being able to tell how fast you are running) and pace familiarization so that you run "under control" and comfortably during the race.

Strength
Strength training for distance runners seeks to improve aerobic capacity (VO2 Max) and reduce lactate levels. To do this, workouts are designed to produce and consume lactate at levels consistent with marathon effort or faster. Ideally, as you get closer to the marathon these workouts should become more specific, done at marathon goal pace. Aerobic capacity and the lactate system are also trained by endurance and pace training.

Glossary of Mystifying Training Terms
All types of training can be categorized into the three types listed above: endurance, strength or pace. However, if you go to your local running club meeting or pick up a copy of a running magazine, you will find many mysterious terms for different forms of workouts. We have included some of these below along with other definitions. We apologize if we have left out anyone's favorite.

Speed Work: a general term for almost any strength or pace training. An integral part of any of these types of workouts is at least 5-10 minutes of warm up and 5-10 minutes of cool-down.

Fartlek: Swedish for "speed play" - a type of training when the runners runs at different paces. Fartlek is often run on hilly courses in which the runner speeds up or slows down at will, with the terrain or on a coaches direction. It can be run on flat terrain by alternating speeding up for a period of time, then slowing down for recovery (Strength Training)

Pace Runs: a continuous short hard paced run. Typically it is run at or near race pace. (Pace Training)

Time Trial: a time trial is used to measure progress and should be run at all out pace for the distance covered. An easy way to run a time trial is to run a short race. The distance of the race should be 10% or less of the weekly mileage to allow reasonable recovery. Although not really training, it has strength training benefits and provides a benchmark for current fitness.

Short Intervals: repeated short periods of work followed by rest intervals of reduced activity. The work intervals are often run near maximum aerobic pace, (2 mile to 10k race pace), and are followed by intervals of recovery, passive to 75% of maximum heart rate or active via a short jog or walk. (Strength Training)

Long Intervals or Repetitions : interval training run near race pace with full recovery to about 60% of maximum heart rate. This type of running is very specific for leg speed. (Pace Training, Strength Training when high volume)

Maximum Heart Rate: maximum heart rate in beats per minute can be estimated by subtracting your age from 220. Accurate maximum heart rates can only be obtained through testing. Testing at max requires the presence of a physician.

Maximum Aerobic Pace: a pace which is scientifically measured by treadmill testing, but can be determined using the 12 minute test or pace for a 2 mile race. The 12 minute test is done on a track or measured course with the distance covered during a 12 minute run divided into the time to give maximum aerobic pace in minutes per mile. Maximum aerobic pace can also be estimated from a 10K or other race time using the tables in the Appendix to estimate a 2 mile race pace.

Hill Repeats: does not mean simply running up hills, but is a specific hill technique. A hill with a gradual 5-10% grade that is 100-300 yards long is used. The runner repeatedly runs or bounds up the hill and strides down the hill as fast as possible (this should include 30-60 seconds of hard running). Uphill develops dynamic power and downhill develops rapid leg movement patterns and stride length. (Strength Training)

Even Effort: a description of pacing that expends energy at a constant rate throughout a run. Best race performance are usually done with even effort A common problem on hills is that runners expend so much energy on the uphill that they cannot use the advantage of the downhill to run faster, but use it to rest. A better plan is to run up and down the hills at the same effort. Then using that effort on the downhill becomes a major advantage. At even effort, uphill is usually run about 10% slower than the flat while downhill is run 5% faster.

Cross Training: training using other types of aerobic activity such as swimming, bicycling, walking or water running. A major value of cross training is injury prevention. The aerobic endurance training may or may not be equivalent. The specificity component is missing depending on the specificity of cross training to running. Part of cardiovascular endurance involves the training of the muscles used for better oxygen utilization through increased aerobic enzymes. This can be done somewhat through cross training, but running is better. Cross training will benefit you especially if you cannot run every day. It will add some variety and help keep you motivated to stay on your training schedule.

Interval Training

Interval training was developed by German physiologists in the 1930's and popularized by the great Hungarian coach Mihaly Igloi. There are 5 variables used in describing interval training:

- The fast run distance
- The fast run pace
- The recovery run distance
- The recovery run activity (slow run vs. walk vs rest)
- The number of repetitions

Manipulating these variables makes interval training adaptable to virtually all types of running. Interval training can be applied very effectively to sprints, middle and long distances. It allows large amounts of work to be done by interspersing it with recovery periods.

Short Intervals

If training for long distance events with minimal energy demands and lactate accumulation, the most suitable use of short interval training is to improve aerobic power and range of motion. The most effective way to do this is to repeat short fast runs close to maximal aerobic pace, (2 mile to 10k race pace). Because this maximal aerobic pace can only be continuously maintained for approximately 2 miles without stopping, breaking the work load into fast run intervals of much shorter duration allow a greater total work load to be completed. Most research indicates fast runs of 200 to 400 meters to be most effective for improving VO2 Max. Because the intent is to maintain the cardiovascular system near its maximum aerobic limit, rest intervals should be short, equal to the fast distance or less and should be run slowly rather than walked to decrease lactic acid buildup in the muscles. The runner's pulse rate should drop to about 75% of maximum during this rest period. The number of repetitions depends on the conditioning of the runner.

A runner starting an interval program should begin with a total fast run duration of less than 1 mile in intervals of 400 meters, (1 lap on a track), or less. When recovery pulse and leg fatigue indicate, more intervals can be added.

Pace Runs

Pace runs are runs done at constant moderate effort, usually at or slightly faster than race pace. These runs have two benefits. First, because they are run near race pace, they are effective physical and mental simulators of a race. The body and mind learn to function efficiently at racing speeds. The neuromuscular communication paths necessary to operate in a race are established. The ability to deal with race levels of lactate is trained. The runner's feel of racing speed is developed as is ability to focus and maintain pace.

Another benefit of pace runs can be derived by running at 85-90% effort for the workout distance. This creates a cardiovascular overload and accompanying strength benefits similar to those derived by aerobic interval training. Optimal pace runs combine both of these effects through an educated selection of a pace run distance of about 1/4 of the race distance. If this distance is run at race pace, it will always be an 85-90% effort run for the workout distance. For the marathon an excellent pace workout is 6-7 miles at marathon race pace. Because of their dual benefits, pace runs are probably the most effective type of speedwork training for the marathon.

Long Intervals or Repeats
Repeats are essentially multiple pace runs combined into an interval training format. The key differences between repeats and short intervals lie in the recovery time, the fast run distance and the pace. Repeats utilize long rest periods during which the runner is allowed to recover fully before doing another fast run. The rest periods often use walking or standing for the intermediate activity. Fast run distances for repeats are usually 800 meters or longer. The fast run pace for repeats is usually race pace or race pace goal. Because work bouts are broken up by rest, repeats allow more pace work to be done than a pace run at the same intensity. Beginners should start with less distance and fewer repeats run at or below their current race pace ability. They can then build up to a maximum of total repeat run mileage equal to around 10% of their weekly mileage base and speed near their goal race pace.

Fartlek
Fartlek is an unstructured form of speedwork often done on varied or cross country terrain. During a moderately paced run, the runner varies his speed by periodically accelerating to harder paces and then slowing back down to an easy pace. The object is to maintain an average level of effort of about 80-85% of race pace. The surges push the effort to 90% or more and the slower paces are a 75-80% effort for recovery. Fartlek is a very effective simulation of passing and surging in races and is useful in building aerobic power and speed especially when done on hilly terrain. It provides a pleasant alternative to structured track interval workouts and provides the extra benefits of running hills and utilizing different muscle groups. Fartlek may be one of the best ways to train the lactate system with the alternate bouts of production and consumption. These bouts should teach the body to produce less and consume more lactate.

Race Specific Training
During the sharpening phase of training, it is important to consider the specifics of the particular race for which you are training. Your training runs should be tailored to simulate as closely as possible the terrain, the surface and environment in which you expect to race.

Sharpening Programs
The following are examples of several programs that can be used to develop a schedule for the sharpening phase of marathon training.

Novice Marathon Sharpening

Prerequisites
Base of 35 miles per week including a long run of between 15 and 20 miles

Goals
To build marathon endurance by completing three 20 mile training runs. To develop marathon pace through short pace runs

Mileage Progression

Week	S	M	T	W	T	F	S	Total
18	16	0	4	8	4	8	0	38
19	20	0	4	8	4	8	0	44
20	16	0	4	2P	4	8	0	38
21	20	0	4	8	4	8	0	44
22	16	0	4	3P	4	8	0	39
23	20	0	4	8	4	8	0	44
24	16	0	4	4P	4	8	0	40
25	16	0	4	6	4	6	0	36

(P) Pace runs consist of:
- 1 mile warm up easy jog
- 4 short intervals of 100 Meter run at 10k race pace, 100 Meter walk*
- 4 short intervals of 200 Meter run at 10k race pace 200 Meter jog*
- A pace run of the indicated number of miles at marathon goal pace*
- 1 mile jog to cool down.

* See Pace Tables in Appendix. On a 400 meter track, 100 meters is approximately the length of the straightaway or curve. 200 meters is a straightaway plus a curve. One mile is approximately 4 laps.

All other runs are done at an easy, (80% effort), training pace.

Beginning Marathon Sharpening

Prerequisites
Base of 40 miles per week including a long run of between 15 and 20 miles

Goals
To build marathon endurance by completing four 20 mile training runs. To develop marathon pace through short pace runs

Mileage Progression

Week	S	M	T	W	T	F	S	Total
18	16	0	4	2P	4	8	0	38
19	20	0	4	8	4	8	0	44
20	16	0	4	3P	4	8	0	39
21	20	0	4	8	4	8	0	44
22	16	0	4	4P	4	8	0	40
23	20	0	4	8	4	8	0	44
24	20	0	4	4P	4	8	0	44
25	16	0	4	6	4	6	0	36

(P) Pace runs consist of:
- 1 mile warm up easy jog
- 4 short intervals of 100 Meter run at 10k race pace, 100 Meter walk*
- 4 short intervals of 200 Meter run at 10k race pace, 200 Meter jog*
- A pace run of the indicated number of miles at marathon goal pace*
- 1 mile jog to cool down.

* See Pace Tables in Appendix. On a 400 meter track, 100 meters is approximately the length of the straightaway or curve. 200 meters is a straightaway plus a curve. One mile is approximately 4 laps.

All other runs are done at an easy, (80% effort), training pace.

Recreational Marathon Sharpening

Prerequisites
Base of 50 miles per week including a long run of 20 miles

Goals
To establish a strong endurance base by completing 6-8 runs of 20 miles or more. To develop marathon pace and aerobic potential through a program of pace runs and intervals

Mileage progression

Week	S	M	T	W	T	F	S	Total
18	20	0	5	2P	5	10	0	46
19	20	0	5	3R	5	10	0	47
20	16	0	5	3P	5	10	0	43
21	20	0	5	3R	5	10	0	47
22	16	0	5	3P	5	10	0	43
23	20	0	5	4R	5	10	0	48
24	20	0	5	4P	5	10	0	48
25	16	0	5	4P	5	8	0	42

(R) Repeat runs consist of:
- 1 mile warm up easy jog
- 4 short intervals of 100 Meter run at 10k race pace, 100 Meter walk*
- 4 short intervals of 200 Meter run at 10k race pace 200 Meter jog*
- Indicated number of 1 mile repeats at marathon goal pace* with standing recovery.
- 1 mile jog to cool down.

(P) Pace runs consist of:
- 1 mile warm up easy jog
- 4 short intervals of 100 Meter run at 10k race pace, 100 Meter walk*
- 4 short intervals of 200 Meter run at 10k race pace, 200 Meter jog*
- A pace run of the indicated number of miles at marathon goal pace*
- 1 mile jog to cool down.

* See Pace Tables in Appendix. On a 400 meter track, 100 meters is approximately the length of the straightaway or curve. 200 meters is a straightaway plus a curve. One mile is approximately 4 laps.

All other runs are done at an easy, (80% effort), training pace.

Intermediate Marathon Sharpening

Prerequisites
Base of 60 miles per week including a long run of 20 miles

Goals
To establish a strong endurance base by completing 6-8 runs of 20 miles or more. To develop marathon pace and aerobic potential through a program of pace runs and intervals

Mileage progression

Week	S	M	T	W	T	F	S	Total
18	22	0	6	3R	6	12	6	59
19	20	0	6	4R	6	12	6	58
20	24	0	6	4P	6	12	6	62
21	20	0	6	5R	6	12	6	59
22	24	0	6	5P	6	12	6	63
23	20	0	6	6R	6	12	6	60
24	22	0	6	6P	6	12	6	62
25	16	0	6	6P	6	10	6	54

(R) Repeat runs consist of:
- 1 mile warm up easy jog
- 4 short intervals of 100 Meter run at 10k race pace, 100 Meter walk*
- 4 short intervals of 200 Meter run at 10k race pace, 200 Meter jog*
- Indicated number of 1 mile repeats at marathon goal pace* with standing recovery.
- 1 mile jog to cool down.

(P) Pace runs consist of:
- 1 mile warm up easy jog
- 4 short intervals of 100 Meter run at 10k race pace, 100 Meter walk*
- 4 short intervals of 200 Meter run at 10k race pace, 200 Meter jog*
- A pace run of the indicated number of miles at marathon goal pace*
- 1 mile jog to cool down.

* See Pace Tables in Appendix. On a 400 meter track, 100 meters is approximately the length of the straightaway or curve. 200 meters is a straightaway plus a curve. One mile is approximately 4 laps.

All other runs are done at an easy, (80% effort), training pace.

Advanced Marathon Sharpening

Prerequisites
Base of 75-80 miles per week including a long run of 24 miles and previous speedwork at marathon race pace or faster

Goals
To establish strong endurance base by completing 8 long runs of between 20 and 30 miles. To peak marathon potential with specific pace runs and intervals

Mileage Progression

Week	S	M	T	W	T	F	S	Total
18	24	7	7	5R	7	14	7	75
19	22	7	7	5P	7	14	7	73
20	24	7	7	6R	7	14	7	76
21	22	7	7	6P	7	14	7	74
22	24	7	7	6R	7	14	7	76
23	22	7	7	6P	7	14	7	74
24	24	7	7	6R	7	14	7	76
25	16	7	7	6P	7	12	7	66

(R) Repeat runs consist of:
- 1 mile warm up easy jog
- 4 short intervals of 100 Meter run at 10k race pace, 100 Meter walk*
- 4 short intervals of 200 Meter run at 10k race pace, 200 Meter jog*
- Indicated number of 1 mile repeats at marathon goal pace* with standing recovery.
- 1 mile jog to cool down.

(P) Pace runs consist of:
- 1 mile warm up easy jog
- 4 short intervals of 100 Meter run at 10k race pace, 100 Meter walk*
- 4 short intervals of 200 Meter run at 10k race pace, 200 Meter jog*
- A pace run of the indicated number of miles at marathon goal pace*
- 1 mile jog to cool down.

* See Pace Tables in Appendix. On a 400 meter track, 100 meters is approximately the length of the straightaway or curve. 200 meters is a straightaway plus a curve. One mile is approximately 4 laps.

All other runs are done at an easy, (80% effort), training pace.

Psychological Preparation

Almost all competitive runners will agree that a major component of their sport is psychological. When we have questioned marathoners at Boston, New York, Twin Cities, Honolulu, Seattle and Portland, the consensus was that more than 50% of competition was psychological. However, very few runners acknowledged that they incorporated psychological training into their programs. We think that this is because few runners understand the concepts of sports psychology much less how to apply them to their training.

During the 1970s it became clear to many researchers in sports science that a significant part of any successful athletic performance was due to psychological factors. Athletes who have been successful in many sports have been studied to determine what psychological traits make them superior. Five significant traits can be identified.

They Know How To Win
Successful athletes set many achievable goals. This goal setting technique does two things. First, it is easy to develop commitment to a goal that is realistic and achievable. Second, if there are many goals, some will always be achieved, guaranteeing success.

Why is success important? Because it builds self esteem and confidence, the bases for vision and self control.

They Make Things Happen
Successful people have an attribute called vision. While most of you like to perform in the area where you have experience and can use the feedback; top performers are able to envision performance outside this "comfort zone". They are able to "push back the envelope". Instead of using terms like "Because" and "That's the way I've always done it", they have the imagination to say "What if" or "Just do it". In order to have a breakthrough performance, it is imperative to have vision. Vision can and does drive performance in all endeavors.

They Love a Challenge
Top performers look at events, barriers, and circumstances as challenges to undertake with an optimistic point of view. Losers see these things as obstacles that cannot be overcome, a pessimistic point of view. The successful athlete knows that positive vision and appraisal drives positive performance. He/she feels in control of any situation and recognizes the importance of facing up to obstacles.

They Control Energy

There are two kinds of energy: positive and negative. Successful athletes can control both kinds of energy to their benefit. They know how and when to apply pressure to themselves and how to control and channel outside energy to their benefit. They also know what motivates them to their best performances. We have heard elite athletes speak of their "moments of doubt" and the techniques they use to turn those into "moments of control".

They Perform in "The Zone"

Just what is "the zone"? When athletes describe top performances no matter what the sport, their descriptions of what they were feeling are very similar. Common thoughts show a combination of relaxation and tremendous energy; enjoyment of the activity without anxiety or fear; an effortless performance. They describe not having to think about what they were supposed to do, but that it came naturally. They were able to concentrate easily and had super awareness. They felt in complete control, able to do anything, confident and positive. Again self-control is an important element.

Goals - Setting Yourself up to Win

The first step to success is learning how to set goals. We have asked hundred of runners in our marathon clinic what got them out the door to do the required training. Over 90% answered that they had committed to the marathon and, thus, needed to do the training.

Goal setting is a behavioral approach to self-control that utilizes setting specific goals and self-reinforcement through their achievement. The achieved goal acts as reinforcement and as a stimulus to pursue the next goal, helping to maintain motivation and build self-confidence. It is an intrinsic reward. Other extrinsic (real) rewards may also help to keep you focused towards achieving a long-term goal.

Goals need to be multiple, achievable, reasonable and definite. We often have runners come to us with too many and too disparate goals such as in the next 2 months I want to run a marathon, set 10K personal bests, race every weekend and only run 10 miles a week. We suggest that you spend some time setting up goals on a seasonal basis. Look at the race calendar for the year, decide how many and what kind of races you want to do. Determine which races are most important to you. You can run a marathon, set 10K bests and finish many races, but not all of these at the same time and not in 2 months.

In a training program, the easiest way to set goals is to lay out a written training program with long term goals, (6- 12 months or more), medium term (4-12) weeks, short term (1-4 weeks) and daily goals. Break the year and the race schedule into training and racing seasons; no one can race well either physically or mentally year round. You can run races year round, but plan to run them only for fun or as a training run during the training season. Next set goals for shorter periods of time. Most runners get into ruts of using mileage and pace as their only goals. Some runs are easy days, so the goal should be to run, relax and enjoy it. Other goals could be to run a different route or to run with a friend. The goal could be to be in control of the pace and run an even effort workout on both hard and easy days. The goal for a training run should be completion as near the target pace as possible given the days conditions. This way, if you stick to your training plan, you will guarantee being a winner if you run the workout.

Keep a training log that has space for planned and actual runs. Record how you feel during each run.

To help you with goal setting you may want to join a training group or get some private coaching.

Talking about your running and training with others runners is a way to maintain commitment. It is important for your family and friends to understand your level of commitment. Communicate to them what your running gives you, how it makes you feel, and, most important, your goals. This sharing will help them understand your need go out the door when time is short, when the weather is bad or your need to run every day.

Vision - Making Things Happen

Vision is a very powerful concept. It has been called various names such as "mind over body" and, more recently, "feedforward".

States of Existence

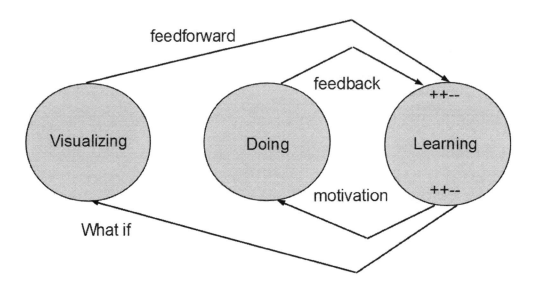

Routinely our existence is within a comfortable action/reaction loop where you are either doing (Action) or learning (Reaction). Learning provides the knowledge or basis for action. If your actions result in positive feedback (i.e. we enjoy the action), you will approach performing the action or activity positively the next time. You will be motivated.

One very strong way you achieve enjoyment from a task is by being successful at doing the task. In other words, success breeds a positive approach to an activity. This positive approach is called confidence. Failure, on the other hand, provides negative feedback and destroys confidence. To maintain and improve commitment, it is imperative for you to be successful, to feel that you are a winner and to build self-confidence and motivation.

With increased levels of self-confidence and motivation comes the courage to "push back the envelope", take risks and extend our horizons. This is always preceded by forward thinking, what we call vision. You can run 2 miles every day, then wake up one morning and think "what if I run 5 miles today". This is vision. It's the courage to extend beyond previous performance levels.

Note again, that our learning provides the knowledge or basis for action. A researcher, Maxwell Maltz, showed that learning takes place even when you are visualizing, just thinking about an activity and not performing it. In short, if the visualization is good enough the brain can't tell whether you are doing, (feedback), or visualizing, (feedforward), and you can learn from it. Since learning drives performance, a positive visualization of a performance can help promote success in an actual performance. This aspect of sports psychology is called "feedforward". Its effectiveness has been demonstrated many times in Olympic training programs of the last 3 decades.

The first step in improving your psychological performance is to be aware of your feelings, thoughts and sensations while you are running. Leave your music player at home and, instead, tune into your own body while running by yourself. Take note of what you are seeing, how you are feeling, and what you are thinking. You will be surprised at the range of your thoughts and emotions.

Simulation greatly enhances the ability to visualize by providing a realistic basis for the vision. Simulation uses practice of desired performance responses and coping strategies in situations as real as you can make them. For the runner, this means that selected competitive situations are reproduced as closely as possible during practice. Introduce yourself to the expected things. Run the race pace; run the race duration; run the race course; run in all kinds of expected weather conditions; practice drinking fluids at specific intervals; run when hungry, after eating, during the expected time of the race (morning, afternoon, etc.), or when you are tired. Then introduce the unexpected. Practice passing people, having others pass you, have your friends come out during your run and say "Looking good" or whatever bothers you.

Human modeling is another form of simulation that attempts to emulate, model or reproduce the positive behavior of another, perhaps highly skilled athlete. Modeling can place you in the position to look at and draw upon other peoples' strengths in order to better your own physical and psychological strengths. For example, watch a video of the Olympic marathons and pretend you're one of the race leaders and imagine yourself running the marathon as they do.

If you want to control your own destiny, you need to know in advance what is expected of you and how you are going to produce it. This requires visualization.

Visualization is a form of simulation that takes place in your head. It gives you a chance to deal with an event or problem internally before you must deal with it in real life. For visualization to work, you must be able to vividly imagine yourself executing the skill or response.

Before some of your workouts, find a quiet place where you can relax and spend 5 - 10 minutes considering the workout. First, acquaint yourself with the workout's requirements: times, distance, etc. Then consider the goals of the workout and what it should do for you physiologically and, possibly, psychologically. Last picture yourself running the workout smoothly over the entire course, finishing within your time window and getting any reward you have planned for yourself. As you get better at doing this, make the visualization as detailed as possible with colors, sounds, smells, and physical sensations of your experience.

Use the same technique while you are doing your workout to periodically visualize the next segment of the workout. If you have trouble, try watching yourself in windows as you pass, following your shadow or by having someone videotape you.

When you are running and are feeling that relaxed, floating, "I could run forever" feeling, try to focus on your mental picture of that effort. Practice seeing that image when you are not running and when you are tired during a run. Use that mental picture to improve the way you feel while you're running.

Self-control - Dealing With Challenges and Focusing Energy

Self-control is important in being able to perform well under a variety of stress-producing circumstances. Some aspects include being able to accept criticism, not being afraid to fail, maintaining composure under stress and being able to perform to potential during competition. To do these you need to be able to control and channel your emotions, focus your concentration, bounce back from setbacks, and most importantly, deal with negative thoughts. Negative thoughts and emotions create negative performances. During competition, they can result in a vicious negative cycle of thought and performance, the destruction of commitment. Most competitive runners have experienced this destructive scenario.

A serious runner should pursue and maintain the attitude of an optimist. Barriers can be viewed as obstacles or challenges. Winners see barriers in their paths as challenges rather than obstacles. People who excel often don't even see the barriers as challenges, but as a normal part of the activity. "Obstacles are what you see when you take your eyes off your goal" - Johnny Danger, motorcycle daredevil. Most barriers faced in competition are the same for all the competitors. Those who use them as challenges they can rise above, rather than as obstacles that hinder performance, will be victors. You can be a winner or a whiner.

Another important part of self-control is controlling and channeling psychological energy. Energy comes in two forms: positive and negative. Positive energy is the energy you get when you are enjoying an activity, e.g. a "slam dunk" in basketball. Negative energy is the energy you get from fear. Both of them can be motivators. Psychological research, however, has shown that the best performances take place in an atmosphere of positive energy, often described by the participants as a state of joy. Although negative energy can motivate you to perform, it is more often associated with negative motivation. Negative thoughts and fears usually inhibit performance rather than drive it. In competition, once doubt gains a foothold, it has a tendency to snowball into many negative thoughts, loss of energy and poor performance. Winners recognize and have ways of dealing with negative thoughts. If possible, they avoid them entirely. Otherwise, they are able to cope with them rapidly and dismiss them.

Try to detect negative thoughts while you are running or thinking about your running. You may wish to write some of them down and think about them later. Many of these negative thoughts can be dismissed immediately as being "plain stupid" or as being about things over which you have no control. Most of the others can be turned into challenges or put into a positive perspective.

Sometimes the key to solving problems is the ability to view things in a rational and constructive manner. One way to do this is to prevent anxiety from arising. Anxiety arises mainly from irrational or illogical beliefs. Some of these beliefs are that you must always have the approval of those you love; that you must do everything extremely well; that you cannot control or change your feelings; or that you must worry about something that seems fearsome or dangerous. The way to reduce unwanted and unproductive anxiety is to challenge and change some of your irrational beliefs and feelings.

Begin change by questioning the thoughts that upset you. Use self-talk to tell yourself new things. Mental imagery can be used to imagine yourself thinking new thoughts and taking differing courses of action in tough situations. Attempt, in your mind, to see yourself thinking, believing and acting in more constructive ways, then try to duplicate this in real life. If a change in perspective or belief is experienced, try to be aware of what you did or said to make it happen and use that pattern again. Sometimes re-labeling or re-interpreting sensations can put you in control. That knot in your stomach before the race could let you say, "I'm so nervous. I hope I don't blow it" or it could signal that your body is saying, "I'm pumped up and ready for action. Let's go!" Thoughts control emotions. Become aware of your thoughts and use them to your advantage.

Having positive or negative energy is one thing; controlling it is another. Winners have the ability to focus the energy into performing the task at hand. Whether it is the dread of a final exam in school or the excitement generated by the crowd at the Boston Marathon, winners know how to use it.

Relaxation

Sometimes you are too tense or too anxious to achieve your best performance. Having the ability to physically relax and calm yourself mentally allows you to reach an optimum level of activation to enhance performance. We all have the body responses to the onset of stress - muscle tenseness, queasy stomach, increased heart rate, etc. Become aware of your body signals and use them as your signals to relax. You can focus on relaxing different muscles in your body. You can use deep breathing. Follow each breath with an effort to relax or use mental imagery to imagine yourself in a relaxed state. There are several relaxation procedures you can learn including progressive relaxation, but all need frequent practice. Relaxation may help you to get a good night sleep before the race as well as during the race.

The most important relaxation tool to learn is deep or diaphragmatic breathing, which can give an immediate sense of relaxation throughout the body while you are running. This type of breathing allows more oxygen to be taken in and get into the blood leading to better physical and mental performance. Diaphragmatic or belly breathing works by the expansion of the lower abdomen creating a vacuum in the chest which causes air to be drawn into the lower lungs. As the middle lungs fill, the upper abdomen expands and finally the chest expands as the upper lungs are filled. To practice, lie on your back with your hands on your abdomen just above your navel. Exhale completely. Inhale through your nose allowing your abdomen to expand. As you fill your lungs completely, exhale through your mouth. Practice by blowing all your air out through your mouth using your abdominal muscles and pushing down with your hands. Then inhale again through your nose filling your lungs completely and exhale by blowing the air out through your mouth. Practice about 5 complete cycles. Note the relaxed feeling throughout your body. This type of breathing is useful while you are running. Concentrate on belly breathing inhaling through both nose and mouth when you begin to feel tired or when you are running uphill. The increased oxygen and relaxed upper body should make the running seem easier.

Focus

Concentration involves changing the focus of attention during the event. Focus is awareness of one thing to the exclusion of others. It must be adjustable from narrow (my calf feels tight) to broad (how hard am I working to run this pace). It is important to learn when each of these is necessary. Interplay of relaxation and focus then becomes a concentration cycle from the mind (seeing yourself running relaxed), to body (relaxing the calf muscle), to target (centering on running this mile). Sometimes learning to shift attention is important to learn to change the focus. Let your mind run free, then bring it back to the necessary focus and repeat the cycle.

Maintaining this focus of energy is one of the most difficult tasks for a long distance runner in competition. You will be faced with numerous energy wasting distractions and negative thoughts during the marathon. To achieve top performance, you must learn to stay positively focused.

On your "hard" workout days, practice detecting your level of focus. You should be thinking in the present about what you are doing, not in the past or the future or about external things.

On your "easy" workout days practice relaxing and dismissing all stress producing negative thoughts you may have. Work on visualizing yourself effortlessly running in a state of enjoyment. Think about "looking good" so if others see you run by they will think you are completely enjoying your run.

Achieving "The Zone"

The ultimate in self-control is when it is totally automatic, the state athletes call being "in the zone". Almost everyone has had an experience when everything seemed to flow like magic and performance was effortless, even joyful. These experiences are often described as "out of body" or "Zen-like" because of the degree of simultaneous focus and awareness and the lack of physical effort to the point that the performance is joyful. The "zone" is mysterious, but it is a place where winners live.

We have no exercises guaranteed to get you into "the zone." It is important for you to recognize when you have these positive psychological experiences and try to determine what led you to them. If you have one, write down in your training log everything you can remember about what happened and what the surrounding conditions and environment were. After several "zone" runs, perhaps you can find a key to what motivates your experience.

Try to recognize "zone" experiences when you are watching others take part in sports. Hang out with runners that you think have achieved running "in the zone".

If you are interested in learning more about sports psychology, read either Peak Performance by Charles A. Garfield or The Warrior Athlete by Dan Millman. Both will give you specific techniques and exercises to help you improve your performance from a psychological focus. Both are excellent, but have slightly different emphasis.

Quick Reference to Psychological Training Techniques

TOOLS
  Have a Training Plan
    - long term goals
    - short term goals
    - strategy

  Keep a Training Log
    - daily plans and goals
    - daily results
    - comments

PRE-WORKOUT
  Revisit Plan and Goal
    - how far
    - how fast
    - what is the purpose of this workout
  Plan Rewards
    - for major workouts
    - for achieving goals
  Visualize Workout as a Positive Experience (2-3 minutes)
    - yourself exercising
    - your route
    - what you feel, see, hear, smell and taste
    - completing as planned
    - any post workout reward

DURING WORKOUT
  Develop Self Awareness
    - listen to body
    - listen to thoughts
  Develop Self Control
    - generate positive thoughts and relaxation
    - deal with negative thoughts and tension
    - focus on the present
    - visualize yourself in the present

AFTER WORKOUT
  Log Results
  Log any possible Positive or Negative Influences
    - plan means of using positives in the future
    - plan ways to cope with or avoid negatives
  Reward Yourself for Accomplishing Major Goals

Peaking

Peaking is the ability to optimize your performance for a particular race or race series. It is both a long and short term mental and physical focus on a goal.

Long term focus involves goal setting 6 or more months in advance and devising a long term training plan. For the marathon, this usually involves a 4 to 6 month stamina and endurance building phase with little or no speed work (base building), followed by a 2-3 month specific endurance speed, terrain and environment training phase (sharpening), followed by a short rest and loading phase (tapering) during the week(s) preceding the event. By devising the long term plan and goals, mental focus is put on the marathon from the outset and training is directed at that goal.

Short term focus begins during the sharpening phase. During this phase, training is directed towards topping off aerobic fitness and simulating race conditions. Marathon specific speed work is utilized, heat acclimatization may be performed and familiarity with the marathon terrain is acquired. During this period, training mileage is not increased but rather it should be reduced when speed work is added. Specificity and, for advanced runners, intensity will be increased. The desired effect is to reach maximal marathon readiness the day of the race, not one week early nor one week late.

Psychological Peaking
The basis for psychological peaking is goal setting, goal achievement and reinforcement throughout the training period. By reaching each goal, intermediate as well as ultimate, along the way to the marathon, you become certain that you are prepared and ready to race when race day arrives. Marathon performances do not happen accidentally, they are designed and built.

Throughout your training period, it is important to visualize what you plan to do in the race. Use your feelings and senses during training to learn how you might feel during the marathon so that you will be prepared for the various phases of the race. Learn to listen to and monitor your body so that you will understand what it is saying.

In the sharpening phase of your program, when the training is highly specific, you should have excellent simulation of the race. This can be enhanced even further running on similar terrain, at the same time of day and even on the marathon course itself. Familiarize yourself with the course so that you can run through the race many times in your mind.

Concentrate on the following tasks while you are doing your training runs:

Know Yourself: learn your body and its responses during training runs. Practice new tactics, eating habits such as carbo loading, and drinking water while on training runs. Learn what motivates you. Use your training diary to learn what factors are associated with best and worst runs (i.e. thinking, focus, what you've eaten, how much rest or sleep you've gotten, etc.). Use your own patterns to your best advantage.

Listen to Your Body: learn to monitor your body signals while you are running. Do body scans or body checks such as "how do my feet feel, are my calf muscles relaxed, is my breathing regular and not too fast, is my upper body tense, are my jaws and teeth clenched".

Talk to Your Body: pick some key words that work for you such as relax, smooth, float or whatever and practice saying and responding to them. Do a body scan and repeat your key word 5-10 times in a row while exhaling.

Listen to Your Mind: learn to detect negative or extraneous thoughts during your training runs and to deal with them. In your hard workouts, learn to focus thoughts and energy into being in control of your runs: not too fast, not too slow, but smooth and perfectly paced. If you learn to control your workouts you will be able to control your race.

Relax: use relaxation techniques to get a good night's sleep, to remain calm, run smoothly and conserve energy during your runs.

Use Visualization and Imagery: before and during your workouts see yourself overcoming challenges and feel yourself running comfortably (smooth, relaxed and in control). Use images of smoothly running animals, relaxed settings or powerful machinery to get body responses. Recall positive experiences from previous training runs or races. Intersperse verbal reminders to drink fluids, maintain pace and focus on form.

Learn to Deal with Discomfort: an adequate training program combined with proper race pacing should prevent intense pain during the marathon. However, pain does sometimes occur. Note the normal sensations of fatigue during your long training runs so that you will know what to expect during the race. Most of what is felt in the marathon is discomfort due to fatigue or simply the sane body talking to the insane master "What are you doing to me, I'm tired". The master can answer, "I'm the master here and I want to finish, it's not much farther, We can do it!"

Simulate Your Race: practice on similar terrain or on the actual course. Learn the best way to divide it into sections. Practice body scans, self-talk and other psychological tools. Use your imagination to see yourself running as a graceful animal, imagine a giant hand pushing you uphill. Run when tired and practice dealing with discomfort. Think of any problems that might arise and figure out how to simulate them and cope with them. Practice racing at your own pace. Practice passing others or having them pass you. The best way to convince yourself that you can do something is to do it. Keep working on the long training runs until you know you can run for the length of time the marathon will take.

Race Preparation

Tapering

The final phase of training is tapering or resting prior to the event. Research has shown that most marathoners start the event overtired. The taper period is important to maximum performance. Each runner responds to tapering approaches differently and there are many personalized schemes used. The following physiological principles apply, however, and should be considered when selecting a tapering method.

- Rebuilding depleted nutrient stores in the body (such as glycogen) to their maximum requires 2 to 3 days of lowered activity.
- Rebuilding minor injuries in muscle or connective tissue takes a minimum of 5 days.
- The body's store of oxidative enzymes diminishes in 72 hours if not stimulated by aerobic exercise.
- Any training effect you get from hard activity during the last 10 days before the race will be minimal.

To summarize the conclusions drawn from all this, you should back off before the event, but not quit running totally. Our recommended approach to marathon tapering is given below. The amount of rest needed depends on the amount of mileage you are running. Beginners and runners with lower mileage take longer to recover and need more rest than runners able to handle more miles. The key to tapering is reducing the distance of the long run with the last extra long run done 2 - 3 weeks before the marathon. The midweek mileage is reduced the last two weeks before the race. Mileage is first reduced to about 75% of the usual and further educed to about 50% the week prior to the marathon. No long run should be done the weekend before the race, instead an easy run of less distance, 8-12 miles, should be run. Studies have shown the importance of doing a small amount of speedwork several days before the race. This keeps you sharp and reinforces the neuromuscular facilitation of marathon pace. The last few days before the marathon, easy workouts of half the normal distance or less should be run. If you normally take the day off before a race and that works well for you, do it. If you are feeling hyper and edgy from the CHO loading and race nervousness, do an easy run of about 10 - 20 minutes.

Carbohydrate loading is an important part of taper with the last three days before the marathon the time for the runner to increase carbohydrate intake while avoiding excess fats and protein. Typical tapering schemes are shown below.

Novice Marathon Tapering

Goals
Last 20 mi. run 3 weeks before to allow complete recovery. Mileage cut to less than half during the last 4 days for rest and carbohydrate loading. Short speedwork to maintain sharpness.

Mileage Progression

```
Week        S       M       T       W       T       F       S          Total

25          16      0       4       6       4       6       0          36
26          8       0       4       2R      2+      2+      0/jog+     22
27          MARATHON
```

The jog is done at an easy pace for about 15 minutes.

(R) Repeat runs consist of:
- 1 mile warm up easy jog
- 4 short intervals of 100 Meter run at 10k race pace, 100 Meter walk*
- 4 short intervals of 200 Meter run at 10k race pace, 200 Meter jog*
- Indicated number of 1 mile repeats at marathon goal pace* with standing recovery.
– 1 mile jog to cool down.

All other runs are done at an easy, (80% effort), training pace.

* See Pace Tables in Appendix. On a 400 meter track, 100 meters is approximately the length of the straightaway or curve. 200 meters is a straightaway plus a curve. One mile is approximately 4 laps.

+Carbohydrate Load

Beginning Marathon Tapering

Goals
Last 20 mi. run 3 weeks before to allow complete recovery. Mileage cut to less than half during the last 4 days for rest and carbohydrate loading. Short speedwork to maintain sharpness.

Mileage Progression

Week	S	M	T	W	T	F	S	Total
25	16	0	4	6	4	6	0	36
26	8	0	4	2R	2+	2+	0/jog+	22
27	MARATHON							

The jog is done at an easy pace for about 15 minutes.

(R) Repeat runs consist of:
- 1 mile warm up easy jog
- 4 short intervals of 100 Meter run at 10k race pace, 100 Meter walk*
- 4 short intervals of 200 Meter run at 10k race pace, 200 Meter jog*
- Indicated number of 1 mile repeats at marathon goal pace* with standing recovery.
– 1 mile jog to cool down.

All other runs are done at an easy, (80% effort), training pace.

* See Pace Tables in Appendix. On a 400 meter track, 100 meters is approximately the length of the straightaway or curve. 200 meters is a straightaway plus a curve. One mile is approximately 4 laps.

+Carbohydrate Load

Recreational Marathon Tapering

Goals
Last 20 mi. run 3 weeks before to allow complete recovery. Mileage cut to less than half during last 4 days for rest and carbohydrate loading. Short tempo run to maintain sharpness.

Mileage Progression

Week	S	M	T	W	T	F	S	Total
25	16	0	5	4P	5	8	0	42
26	8	0	5	2R	2+	2+	0/jog+	23
27	MARATHON							

The jog is done at an easy pace for about 15 minutes.

(R) Repeat runs consist of:
- 1 mile warm up easy jog
- 4 short intervals of 100 Meter run at 10k race pace, 100 Meter walk*
- 4 short intervals of 200 Meter run at 10k race pace, 200 Meter jog*
- Indicated number of 1 mile repeats at marathon goal pace* with standing recovery.
- 1 mile jog to cool down.

(P) Pace runs consist of:
- 1 mile warm up easy jog
- 4 short intervals of 100 Meter run at 10k race pace, 100 Meter walk*
- 4 short intervals of 200 Meter run at 10k race pace, 200 Meter jog*
- A pace run of the indicated number of miles at marathon goal pace*
– 1 mile jog to cool down.

All other runs are done at an easy, (80% effort), training pace.

* See Pace Tables in Appendix. On a 400 meter track, 100 meters is approximately the length of the straightaway or curve. 200 meters is a straightaway plus a curve. One mile is approximately 4 laps.

+Carbohydrate Load

Intermediate Marathon Tapering

Goals
Last 20 mi. run 3 weeks before to allow complete recovery. Mileage cut to less than half during last 4 days for rest and carbohydrate loading. Short tempo run to maintain sharpness

Mileage Progression

Week	S	M	T	W	T	F	S	Total
25	16	0	6	6P	6	10	6	54
26	10	0	6	2R	3+	3+	0/jog+	28
27	MARATHON							

The jog is done at an easy pace for about 15 minutes.

(R) Repeat runs consist of:
- 1 mile warm up easy jog
- 4 short intervals of 100 Meter run at 10k race pace, 100 Meter walk*
- 4 short intervals of 200 Meter run at 10k race pace, 200 Meter jog*
- Indicated number of 1 mile repeats at marathon goal pace* with standing recovery.
- 1 mile jog to cool down.

(P) Pace runs consist of:
- 1 mile warm up easy jog
- 4 short intervals of 100 Meter run at 10k race pace, 100 Meter walk*
- 4 short intervals of 200 Meter run at 10k race pace, 200 Meter jog*
- A pace run of the indicated number of miles at marathon goal pace*
– 1 mile jog to cool down.

All other runs are done at an easy, (80% effort), training pace.

* See Pace Tables in Appendix. On a 400 meter track, 100 meters is approximately the length of the straightaway or curve. 200 meters is a straightaway plus a curve. One mile is approximately 4 laps.

+Carbohydrate Load

Advanced Marathon Tapering

Goals
Last long run 2 weeks before to allow complete recovery. Mileage cut to less than half during last 4 days for rest and carbohydrate loading. Some short accelerations in the workout 4 days before marathon to keep legs loose.

Mileage Progression

```
Week        S       M       T       W       T       F       S         Total

25          16      7       7       6P      7       12      7         66
26          10      7       7       2R      3+      3+      0/jog+    36
27          MARATHON
```

The jog is done at an easy pace for about 15 minutes.

(R) Repeat runs consist of:
- 1 mile warm up easy jog
- 4 short intervals of 100 Meter run at 10k race pace, 100 Meter walk*
- 4 short intervals of 200 Meter run at 10k race pace, 200 Meter jog*
- Indicated number of 1 mile repeats at marathon goal pace* with standing recovery.
- 1 mile jog to cool down.

(P) Pace runs consist of:
- 1 mile warm up easy jog
- 4 short intervals of 100 Meter run at 10k race pace, 100 Meter walk*
- 4 short intervals of 200 Meter run at 10k race pace, 200 Meter jog*
- A pace run of the indicated number of miles at marathon goal pace*
– 1 mile jog to cool down.

All other runs are done at an easy, (80% effort), training pace.

* See Pace Tables in Appendix. On a 400 meter track, 100 meters is approximately the length of the straightaway or curve. 200 meters is a straightaway plus a curve. One mile is approximately 4 laps.

+Carbohydrate Load

Carbohydrate Loading

You have learned about the major energy sources and have, hopefully, experienced using them in running. Your training experience has lead you to run better on fat metabolism and store more carbohydrates (CHO) or glycogen to be used. You also remember that glycogen metabolism must be happening for fat metabolism to easily occur. It is possible to store even more carbohydrates through a process called carbohydrate loading. Normal stores will last for 1 1/2 to 2 hours of running, but CHO loading can be a useful tool for events that last longer than this such as the marathon. You should have been practicing CHO loading throughout your training by consuming a high CHO diet on a regular basis.

Carbohydrate loading has been studied intensely by many exercise physiologists. The original plan involved a six day program with a 3 day depletion phase which could trigger super compensation by the muscles to store glycogen. David Costill, Ball State Human Performance Lab, has done extensive studies to show that an intensely training endurance athlete depletes his muscles to low levels daily and does not need dietary induction of the depletion phase. This athlete normally needs a high CHO diet to replenish his/her muscles. Costill's studies showed that eating a high CHO diet (70%) following a normal 60% CHO diet leads to almost the same muscle glycogen stores as 70% CHO following 15% CHO (depletion phase). The high CHO diet must be accompanied by a reduction in exercise. This information leads us to the following recommended loading scheme.

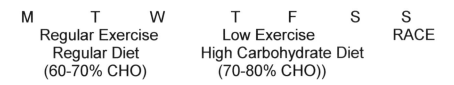

M	T	W	T	F	S	S
Regular Exercise			Low Exercise			RACE
Regular Diet			High Carbohydrate Diet			
(60-70% CHO)			(70-80% CHO))			

Costills' research has also revealed that for over 48 hours of loading, complex carbo's produce greater muscle glycogen storage than simple carbohydrates. The daily requirement for protein and fat should be fulfilled, but the more carbohydrate eaten, the more that will be stored. Storage is facilitated by large meals rather than smaller ones. Our recommended plan is:

- Carbohydrate load for 3 days before the event accompanied by a period of reduced exercise.

- The first day of loading is the most important. Begin with a big carbo breakfast , such as pancakes or French toast. This is the day for the traditional pasta dinner of spaghetti and bread. Try to stuff in as many complex carbohydrates as possible in these two meals.
- Taper off bulk and switch to more simple CHO's as the days progress. Do not load on large quantities of fruit or any other foodstuffs that you don't normally eat.
- Each gram of CHO stores with 3 grams of water. Increase fluid intake to facilitate the CHO storage. Drink an extra 4 - 8 glasses of water and limit dehydrating fluids such as alcohol and caffeine.
- Make certain you are not depleting sodium and potassium stores by drinking too much water. Salt you food and/or include some salty snacks such as pretzels. Eat some fruit including bananas.
- The last major meal should be 12-15 hours before the race and should not include too much bulk. It should be easily digestible so that it will pass through your system before the race. Experiment with this meal before your long training runs so that you know what and how much of the desired food works best for you. We have found 1 or 2 bean burritos with a little cheese works well for us. We always take our own pre race dinner with us after bad experiences from eating untried food in strange restaurants.
- If you plan to eat on race day morning and are used to doing so, a 300-400 calorie high CHO meal such as toast, bagel or oatmeal may be consumed 2-4 hours before the race along with 2 -3 glasses of water. This meal is certainly a matter of personal preference and should be done only if this is usual for you. You can include coffee in your breakfast if you normally drink it. If your race is midday or later, remember to consume a 500-600 calorie breakfast 4 –5 hours before and add a small snack about an hour before. No simple sugars or fruits should be ingested within 1 hour of the run; this could lead to an blood insulin reaction causing weakness and fatigue. If you need something sweet, eat it within 5 - 10 minutes before the start to avoid to avoid an insulin reaction. Drink another 1 - 2 glasses of water in this 5 -10 minute pre race period.

How will you know if you are effectively loading? If you are keeping a record of your daily weight, you will notice a 2-5 or more pound weight gain over the 3 day period. As the CHO is stored, water is also stored in the muscle leading to the weight gain. This water storage may make your legs feel sluggish during your few miles of easy runs, but it may well come in handy during the marathon as a source of sweat etc. You may also feel sleepy, cranky or tired due to the blood sugar and insulin responses to all the carbohydrate. During the race however, you should feel super powered and ready to go.

Carbohydrate loading without the depletion phase should be safe for most healthy individuals. Diabetics and others with particular health problems should consult their physicians before any radical diet changes.

Planning Your Race

The biggest problem may be to decide whether you should run. You may feel unprepared, have an injury, have an illness or other similar problems. You, of course, must make the decision. Even though not running may be a major disappointment, remember that there are lots of other marathons, your training will last for a while and you can easily continue to build on what you've already achieved. One race is never worth a major permanent injury. If you feel unprepared, you can run slower than you planned, run just part of the race or postpone competition until a future event.

Strategies and Tactics

Long before you toe the starting line, you should have an overall strategy for the race. As a minimum, your finish goal, time splits, the number of aid stops and type of aid you will take should be planned in advance. Contingency plans for adverse weather and other conditions also should be considered. Once you have established the race plan, the race itself should be reduced to a series of bite sized goals leading to your finish goal.

Marathon Goals

Set a series of goals for your marathon. Set at least one time goal for the marathon that you know you can accomplish. We recommend setting 3 time goals:

- **Primary** - The one you trained for and think you can accomplish.
- **Contingency** - A goal you will still be happy with under challenging conditions.
- **Ultimate** – A goal you could imagine if everything went perfectly.

These time goals need not and should not be too far apart (5 -10 minutes or so.)

Often runners get so caught up in finish times that they forget there are other important accomplishments. For your first marathon, the main goal should be to finish. Other goals can include learning about marathoning and yourself, to have a good time, to stay injury free, to enjoy running with others and any other goals that are important to you.

Setting a Reasonable finish Time Goal

In a marathon, there are three things that determine how fast you can run: your aerobic potential, your endurance and your experience. Your aerobic potential can be determined from your performances at shorter races and extrapolated to give you a reasonably accurate idea of your marathon potential. One simple way to do this is to take a current race time and use the Pace Tables in the Appendix to estimate your potential marathon time. A 40 minute 10K performance would lead to a 3:07 marathon while a 50 minute 10K predicts a 3:54 marathon. The training pace charts in the appendix give goal times and paces based on various race times. The time you get will be a reasonable estimate of the best time you could run for a marathon given your current aerobic fitness.

Now the bad news, unless you are an experienced marathoner with adequate endurance training, you will find it difficult to run a marathon at your potential. This is because a marathon has specific physical and mental endurance requirements that are only obtained through proper training and experience. (See the previous sections on specificity and endurance training).

Without these, you can expect degradation of 5-10% from the best time estimate given above. If you feel that you don't have enough endurance training or you have never run a marathon, set your finish time goal 10% or so slower than the best time estimate. We see that most beginners finish 5 – 20 minutes slower than the best predicted time and suggest beginners take this into account when setting their time goals. It is much more enjoyable to finish strongly than to experience the sensations people have variously described as "hitting the wall", "being jumped by a bear", "crashing" or "dying". The beginner's first and foremost goal should be to finish!

Splits

To provide sub goals, and to monitor your progress along the racecourse, you should compute a series of intermediate times or "splits" and write them down on something that can be carried along.

Although it is generally accepted that more even splits (constant pace) provide the best results, some runners prefer to use negative (start slow, finish fast) or positive (start fast, finish slow) techniques.

Those using negative splits usually describe races where the technique has been effective as being very positive psychologically because they feel stronger than everyone else at the end. It is a major boost to pass people during the last few miles. For some runners this self-reinforcement may aid performance enough to compensate for the slow start.

Positive splits ("money in the bank" or "kamikaze" approaches) are used as a strategy by some competitive runners to force the pace of their opponents. Running much faster than your average pace at the beginning of a long distance event will almost certainly result in early glycogen depletion and unpleasant feelings. Because some seasoned runners are very good at dealing with these feelings, they can use this as a winning strategy. However, knowledgeable runners seldom use positive splits as a strategy for running the best time. They must be avoided at all costs by beginners. Running faster at the start because you will slow down at the end is a "self fulfilling prophecy". Don't let this happen to you, do the suggested pace training so that you can start out at the proper pace.

Write down your splits and carry them with you. The difficulty of performing high-level math in your head while running in a race is well established. Splits can be written on wristbands, upside down on your race number or on various parts of your body with indelible ink. (Make certain that the ink or paper used is sweat and waterproof). Many marathons print projected race splits that take into account the course terrain.

The splits recommended here are for even effort. On a flat marathon course, you can calculate your average pace per mile by dividing your finish goal time by 26.22. By multiplying the pace per mile by the distance, you can determine target split times for different distances along the course. You should figure out, at least, each of the first 3 miles and the 5, 10, 15, 20 and 25 mile splits. This will allow you to confirm proper pace early and then to check your progress along the way. If you have trouble maintaining a specific pace, you may want to check your splits every mile. If the course has hills, you should not maintain a constant pace. Your splits should allow for even effort, which is slowing down on uphill and speeding up on downhill sections. A good rule of thumb for uphill of 100 feet/mile gain is to add 20 to 30 seconds/mile to your average pace while on steep uphill of 200 ft/mi add 40 to 70 seconds/mile. For downhill, subtract 15 to 20 seconds/mile for 100 ft/mi and 20 to 40 seconds for 200 ft/mi.

Course Knowledge
Many races have been won and lost because of course knowledge. These include examples as catastrophic as getting lost and as simple as having the inside position on the last turn before the finish. The last thing you want during a race is a surprise. Even good surprises have negative consequences and may leave you wondering if you could have done better if you had only known....

Knowledge of a race course can be divided into 3 pieces, the start, the main body of the course and the finish. Knowledge of the course can be obtained in the weeks prior to the race by careful study of the information on the event website such as maps, topographical drawings, pictures, films and talking with others who have been on the course or better yet, by going over the course yourself by car, bicycle or on several early training runs. The important things to determine are the location and degree of any obstacles such as hills, tight turns or constricted areas and the location of dominant landmarks such as turn around points, aid stations, and points where you might want split times. Other items to consider are the type of surface you will be running on and exposure to potential winds, sun, rain etc. If you can, check out the course at the same time of day that the race will occur.

Some event sites have maps or descriptions of the start and finish areas, many do not. If possible, these areas should be viewed before the race for their general features and terrain. Knowledge of the finish may mean the difference between winning and losing precious seconds toward a personal or age group record. You should know exactly where the finish is and exactly when you could start to sprint if you wanted to. Notice if there is a turn or corner just before the finish and how far it is from this to the line. If there are turns near the finish, determine the best position to be in going through them (i.e. the route giving the shortest distance to the finish).

Other Plans

A planned race has the best chance of being a successful race. Your goals should be determined in advance, with the training phases physically and psychologically geared for successful accomplishment of the goal. Last minute changes usually lead to disaster. However, if you wake up with a cold or the outside temperature is 15 - 20 degrees higher than you expected, lowering your goal could be the best plan.

Planing the race includes knowing other aspects such as:

- Exactly where the race starts and finishes.
- How long it takes to get from your house or hotel to the race and how long it takes to find a parking place.
- The locations of the bathrooms at the start and along the course.
- The place to leave and retrieve your warm-ups.
- The location of aid stations and the types of aid available.
- The place to meet your family or friends.

We have included a checklist of items you should need on race day. Use this and add anything else you might need. Plan your clothing needs by keeping weather differences in mind. The shoes you are going to wear should not be brand new, but should have been worn several times and be comfortable. Prepare, lay out or pack these items from a list ahead of time so you can just walk out the door for the race and know that you are prepared.

Checklist for the Marathon
____Shoes
____Insoles
____Orthotics
____Socks
____Shorts
____Singlet
____Underwear
____Watch
____Short sleeved T-shirt
____Long sleeved T-shirt
____Running Tights
____Jacket and Pants (either wind or warm up)
____Visor, hat, sweatband or kerchief
____Gloves or Mittens
____Change of clothes for afterwards
____Number and/or chip if picked up early
____Safety pins
____Course Map
____Race Instructions
____Splits
____Felt tip or ballpoint pen
____Paper tape, bandaids
____Athletic tape
____Skin lubricant
____Powder
____Deodorant
____Sunscreen
____Sunglasses
____Towel
____Prerace food and fluids
____Postrace food and fluids
____Money

Rest and Adaptation
Adequate rest and sleep is extra important in the tapering phase. The most important night's sleep seems to be two nights before the race. Plan your week's schedule accordingly. If you are sleepless the night before the race, don't worry, so are most others. Many records have been set with little or no sleep the night before.

If you are traveling to the race, we suggest that you arrive early in the day preceding it. Review the course if possible. We have found that arriving several days to a week ahead in a different time zone or environment throws you completely off schedule without allowing adequate time to adjust. Arriving the day before seems to be extremely important if traveling to either high altitude or a hot climate. Best performances without adaptation at altitude are within 24-48 hours of arrival. Some short-term adaptation takes place in the first 24 hours, but performance declines are noted in the period between 2 days and 1 month after arrival. Arriving several days early in a hot climate may dehydrate you before the race.

Racing

Final Preparation

"NO NEW IS GOOD NEW." Race time is the time for tried methods, foods, shoes, and equipment. Never try anything for the first time in a race.

Race Morning
Most races have early morning starts. Set your alarm to wake up early so you have plenty of time before the race. You need to be awake and alert. It is also important to get your body functioning and have a bowel movement to get rid of last night's final carbohydrates. Sometimes drinking 1-2 cups of warm water or coffee will assist in this process. If the race starts later in the day, make sure you relax until race time and keep your hydration level up and snack on some easy to digest carbohydrates. Eating on race day was covered in the carbohydrate loading section.

Getting Ready
Your final plans for clothes and shoes will actually depend on the weather. Remember that you will probably be running faster than in training runs; dress accordingly. Too many or too few clothes may be detrimental to performance. The ideal condition is to feel slightly chilly when lined up for the start. The ideal race temperature has been shown to be 55 degrees Fahrenheit for someone running in shorts and a singlet. Below this wearing layers that can be removed is appropriate.

Your race number must always be worn on the front. You may want to fold it to fit on your shorts so you can take off shirt layers if necessary. Pin it on your clothing the night before the race. If there is a removable tag, be sure it is free so that it can be removed at the finish. Most races now use chips that can be detected by sensors along the course. These are either attached to your foot or to the race number itself. Follow the instructions for activating and/or attaching the chip. Otherwise, you may not get a finish time.

The choice between training and racing shoes for the marathon is certainly up to the individual. If you're experienced and race often, you may feel racing shoes give you an added edge. If you're not used to racing flats, their lack of cushioning and/or support over 26 miles may not compensate for the few ounces of reduced weight. To prevent the infamous "black toe" and other foot problems, shoes should have at least a thumb's width of length beyond your longest toe when standing. You should have run several long runs in your shoes prior to the marathon.

Preventing chafing over the marathon distance is important. Vaseline, Body Glide or other athletic skin lubricant can be put wherever 2 body surfaces will rub together or where the edge or seam on clothing will rub on the skin. Paper surgical tape over nipples is a good idea especially for men or when running in the rain. Women should wear the same type of bra worn in training. Powder in the shoes or Vaseline or powder on the feet can reduce blisters and hot spots. Remember to experiment with any of these ideas on long training runs well before the race.

Pick up gear assembled from the checklist and leave for the race giving yourself enough time to park, check on details, warm up and get ready to run.

Before the Start
After arriving, note:

- The location of the bathrooms. Nervousness may lead to several visits. Get in line early, there's usually a crowd.
- Where to put and retrieve your warm-ups.
- Where to meet your companions.
- The location of the finish area, if it is adjacent to the start. Try to get some knowledge of the finish chute system. Some races use different chutes for different ages, sexes or concurrent events. Find out which chute you must use and exactly where the line is relative to the chute, banners or other landmarks.

Warming Up
Warming up before the event has both physiological and psychological benefits. Physiologically. the increased blood flow and muscle core temperature can be beneficial as can the facilitation and recruitment of the motor units. Warm up may help you to prevent injury during the run by having your body prepared and ready to go. Psychologically, it may help you to become clearly focused on the event and on your body. It may burn off a little of the pre-race "hype" and allow you to run the first mile at or near the desired split time. Often being in the crowd and being primed and ready to go can make you go crazy the first mile and run 30 seconds to a minute per mile faster than you wanted. This burns off glycogen that will be needed later. Be warned that warming up might also make it easy to run the first mile too fast because you are loose. Establishing a routine of pre-race activities that become "automatic" can also help calm you.

Use a walk to slow jog to warm up the muscles and the core temperature slowly without causing fatigue or reducing energy stores. Start walking/jogging about 20-30 minutes before the race starts. Slowly move from jog to run, run for 5 to 10 minutes, and then carefully do some easy dynamic exercises. These can include 4-5 short runs of 50 yards or so at marathon pace, skipping, jogging in a tight figure 8, etc. Do not do static stretches before the race, since they will relax your muscles rather than get them primed for racing. Warm up in your warm up clothing and slowly peel down as you get warmer. Warming up should also give you an idea of the amount of clothing necessary for the run. If the temperature is moderate to cool, you should feel chilly while standing in the staging area. If you are comfortable, you either are wearing too many clothes or will need to deal with hot weather running. Relax the last 5 minutes in your starting location. Mentally rehearse starting out slowly, relaxed and under control

Race Tactics

Starting
Your start should be planned to provide the shortest, most obstacle free route to the first turn, if there is one. Start toward the side of the road in the direction of the first turn. If the course narrows appreciably after the start, by design or due to parked vehicles, you may want to start more toward the middle of the road. Find out whether runners are to be seeded by pace and, if so, position yourself toward the front of your pace group at the start. In some races, there are signs indicating pace or finish time goals. If there is no seeding system, get far enough forward in the pack to be near runners of your ability. You can usually tell by their appearance. When in doubt, ask people around you how fast they plan to run. Avoid positioning yourself near runners of vastly different abilities. This usually results in a certain amount of jostling at the start and the potential of someone falling and getting trampled.

While waiting for the gun, you may want to use relaxation techniques to stay calm. It is extremely important not to get too nervous and lose control at the start. Visualize yourself starting at a relaxed controlled pace.

When the gun goes off, start concentrating on the task at hand. Relax, find a clear spot in which to run and establish your pre-planned race pace. It is very easy to run too fast at the start. If you feel like you are running smoothly at an easy training pace, your speed is probably just right!

The First 10 Miles
If you have trained adequately and are healthy, the first 5 to 10 miles should seem very easy to you. You must maintain self control and stick to your race plan. Many runners pass this time socializing with others. During this period of the race you want to establish a rhythm of pace, taking aid and meeting intermediate goals. Use concentration cycles to monitor these items and your various body sensations. Lock yourself into a smooth relaxed stride.

The Second 10 Miles
Somewhere in the second ten miles, runners start to get more serious about the marathon. Socializing will abate some as inner concentration cycles and focus become more important. This is the time the physical and mental simulation you practiced and your experience with long runs will begin to yield returns as you pass goal after goal just as if you've done it all before. Use self-talk to maintain your concentration.

The Last 6 Miles
This is by far the most demanding part of the marathon. If you have prepared adequately and followed your race plan, you should have no difficulty. You will feel fatigue, muscle tightness and soreness during this stage. You may also go through psychological highs and lows. None of these things should surprise you. You have experienced similar feelings on your long training runs and know that they are normal. Encourage yourself with self-talk. Imagery can be used to advantage during this stage to maintain and even lengthen your stride. Picture yourself running as smoothly and effortlessly as you were running at the start of the race.

Somewhere during the last six miles, you will realize that you are going to finish! This usually gives you a big lift. Use it to help you. Start thinking of all the rewards at the finish line and how you will enjoy yourself after the race. Start congratulating yourself. You deserve it! But, don't lose concentration on the goal. If you feel yourself losing focus, try concentrating on keeping your form smooth and relaxed.

Finishing
Make sure you run all the way through the finish line at the end of the race. Run until someone stops you or gives you a medal. Try to keep walking through the chute, stopping immediately drops blood pressure and gives rise to nausea. If event is not chip timed, try to stay in finish order and keep the other runners in order, this helps the race director give correct times and places to the runners.

If you can, do some kind of cool down, either an easy jog or a walk of 10 minutes or so to allow your blood pressure to return to normal and your muscles to cool down. Do not stop abruptly or sit or lay down. This may lead to a rapid drop in blood pressure, possible fainting, leg cramps, and/or nausea. Do not stretch. Stretching exhausted muscles is a sure way to injure them. Ice any areas that are sore by massaging them for about 10 minutes with a block of ice or ice cubes or wrap them with ice packs. You can usually find a medical facility near the finish where you can obtain ice and elastic wraps. Avoid getting in hot water for extended periods after the race as it may cause swelling. A hot shower is OK. A long soak in the hot tub may feel good at the time but may result in swelling in the muscles or joints making them feel sore.

Drink fluids, especially ones rich in electrolytes such as orange juice, tomato juice or sports drink containing electrolytes. You can drink a few beers now using them as a reward and to relax aching muscles. To maintain hydration, drink an equal amount of water with your beer. It is also necessary to keep drinking water throughout the rest of the day. Drink at least one glass every 1-2 hours. Keep drinking until you urinate and your urine is light colored. Eat some food; pick whatever looks good. A large balanced meal may be the best since it will probably contain some of everything you need to replace.

Other Tips and Tactics

Remarkable as it seems, many runners complete 26.2 miles and miss important standards such as Olympic Trial Qualification by only 1 or 2 seconds. Could they have run faster? Probably. How? By paying attention to small details throughout the race. These are the things that experienced road racers do automatically.

Cutting Corners

First of all, this is not cheating. The only racecourses that are "guaranteed" to be accurate are those that are "certified". In this country, courses are certified by the USATF (USA Track & Field) to meet international standards set by the IAAF (International Amateur Athletic Federation). The IAAF and USATF require that courses be measured over the shortest route open to the runners. This means that the course is measured on a route which cuts all corners as closely as possible to the inside apex, usually within 6 inches of the road edge. You are cheating yourself if you do not cut the corners as the course was measured. If you run down the center of the road, each right angle turn will cost you about 1 second in your finish time. To further ensure that courses are not short, the USATF recommends all courses be set up to be 0.1% long, about 50 yards or 8-16 seconds in a marathon.

To run the shortest route, keep as close as possible to the inside edge of the road on all turns and as you come out of the turn assume a straight line route to the inside of the next turn.

Drafting

Many of the current world records for sprinting events in track and field were set at high altitude. The reason for this is the reduction in wind resistance afforded by the "thinner" air. Unfortunately, long distance aerobic events suffer at high altitude because of the lowered ability of the body to transport oxygen to the working muscles. However, even at sea level, a significant reduction in wind resistance can be achieved by a technique known as drafting. As you move through the air, you create a pocket of air behind you that is traveling at the same speed you are. Anyone behind you who is in this pocket does not have to push any air out of the way since it is already moving at his speed. In tests done on bicyclists, it has been shown that nearly 70% of the energy used at 10 miles/hour is due to wind resistance. Bicycling is much more efficient than running. However, a significant reduction in effort on the order of 1-2% can still be realized by drafting when you run, especially into a headwind (wind resistance goes up with the square of the wind speed).

The pocket of air where drafting is effective forms a wedge trailing off at 45 degrees from a runner's shoulder and is probably effective 1 or 2 yards behind him. This means you have to run close to someone, close enough to step on his heels or right on his shoulder and slightly behind him. If you can find 3 or 4 or more runners in a close pack, tuck in behind them for a really good draft.

Be warned that some runners do not like to be drafted especially into headwinds where you are getting an obvious advantage. In this situation, you might best offer to trade off the lead every mile or so with one or more runners so that everyone can benefit.

Clustering

Besides drafting, research on marathoners has determined that running in groups (called clustering) consistently results in better performance than running alone. The benefits are due to group pacing (someone always feels like maintaining the pace), and the group dynamics of sharing the goal and motivating each other.

Taking Aid

Some runners still refuse to stop at aid stations for fear of losing precious seconds. In a marathon, it is absolutely critical that you get enough fluids. Dehydration may cause you to slow significantly in the latter stages of the race or drop out entirely with cramps or sickness. You can get enough fluids at aid stations yet still not lose time if you practice drinking, and you drink and use the aid stations efficiently. Some people are good at running with cups of water in their hands, other spill most of it. If you are a spiller, learn how to chug the water down rapidly or walk through the aid station. Often aid stations are long enough to drink twice while you are passing through them.

Most of the large marathons have aid stations every mile or two. This means you can get enough fluids without drinking as much at each aid station if you chug some (at least 6 oz) at every station. You will probably drop some, but this will help cool you. If all else fails, stop and walk if that is what is necessary to get an adequate supply of fluids during the run. The short walk may break up the tension in your muscles; help you to feel better and ready to run again.

Start drinking fluids at the first aid station. Pick up 1 or more cups at each aid station; pour any extra water over your head and shoulders if you need more cooling. You need at enough water to replace your sweat loss with 4-8 ounces every 20 minutes a reasonable amount. Start ingesting the CHO replacement early. While the carbohydrate can be used immediately, its best usage is 60-90 minutes after ingestion. The electrolytes in the fluid will allow the water and CHO to be absorbed better. We usually alternate water and replacement fluids at the aid stations if they are close together. You should drink 2-4 cups of CHO fluid per hour. If using gels or other concentrated form of CHO's, make certain you get in enough fluids to allow the stomach to empty. Too much or or taken in too high concentration, CHO's may lead to nausea. Fluids taken in the last few miles of the race will probably not be used. However, stopping at the last few aid stations can sometimes help psychologically.

Recovery

After Your Race

What you do the first few hours and days after a marathon is as important as what you do immediately preceding it. This period is critical to your recovery and your future running. The best aid to recovery is a good training program before the marathon. A training program with a good mileage base leads to faster recovery. If you run the marathon without adequate preparation (in spite of all our suggestions), you will suffer both during and after it. If you train well you can cope with the race and will recover faster.

Recovery Factors

There are a number of factors that are important in recovery. The most important of these are muscle soreness, fatigue and feelings of depression. The recovery period and activities should take these items into account. Some general recommendations will be given. These will be followed by recovery progressions.

Delayed muscle soreness after exercise has been described often. The soreness is a feeling of stiffness and soreness that begins 8 or more hours after exercise and may last 3-4 days.(sometimes a week) Researchers propose several causes:

- Damage to the muscle tissue itself. May be due to depletion of energy reserves or actual degeneration of muscle fibers.
- Accumulation of fluid and breakdown products in the muscle.
- Muscle spasm.
- Overstretching or tears of the connective tissue.

The soreness may be a result of one or more of these causes depending on the individual, his state of training and the activity. It is more common after eccentric muscle contraction which is using the muscle in a lengthened state as in downhill running and when dehydration occurs. The most likely causes after a marathon are depletion of energy reserves and the accumulation of fluid in the muscles.

Pain relief can be aided by icing, massage, light activity and slow gentle stretching. All of these things work by increasing the circulation to the area. The increased circulation takes away waste and extra fluid and brings new nutrients. Drinking fluids will help flush the waste products from the body.

Recovery Immediately After the Marathon
A cool down after finishing is important. It may be difficult to do this depending on the finish area. Try an easy jog or a walk of 10 minutes or so. Fainting, leg cramps, and/or nausea may result from stopping suddenly or lying down. Do not stretch now. Your muscles are exhausted and you may activate the stretch reflex leading to cramping or injury. Use massage only if you have previously done that post event. Ask for ice to massage or pack around any sore areas. Drink lots of fluids, especially ones rich in electrolytes such as orange juice or tomato juice. Try to drink at least one glass of water every 1-2 hours. Eat something as soon as you can. Many marathons provide "goodie" bags or meals for finishers; take advantage of these. A large balanced meal may be the best since it will probably contain some of everything you need to replace. Avoid long soaks in hot water that may cause swelling and exacerbate delayed muscle soreness. If you feel like you need a nap, reward yourself with one. Try to take a 10 to 15 minute walk later in the afternoon to keep circulation going and repeat icing of any sore areas.

The Day After the Marathon
Post race depression is quite common. You usually feel a real "high" after finishing especially if you've done well and can talk to other runners and share experiences. The next morning the fatigue and soreness may make you wonder if the marathon was worth it. This letdown is a normal response to meeting your goal and not having a new one. Don't make any plans or predictions until the end of the week. Take time to assess your performance, see if you followed your plan and write down both the good and the bad things that happened. Review your training diary to see what worked well for you and try to pick out any mistakes. Every marathon should be a "learning experience".

Any exercise you can do will promote circulation and aid healing and recovery. If you feel like you can run, find a flat soft surface such as a track. Start slowly; you may be quite stiff. After walking a short distance, your legs should loosen up and running will feel better. This sensation will persist until your muscles start to fatigue and then they will start to stiffen back up. When you feel this begin to happen or if something hurts, you've had enough. When in doubt, don't run any more than you did the day before the marathon (about 10 to 15 minutes). If you feel too sore or stiff to run, take a walk or ride your bike or go swimming for 20 to 30 minutes to get your blood flowing. If anything hurts, ice it after your workout. The long soak in the tub may be OK to take today if nothing is sore. Eat anything that looks or sounds good to you. You probably need it and you certainly deserve it. Your whole body will feel fatigued; plan to take it easy and go to bed early.

The Week After the Marathon

You may experience a general lack of energy the following week. The reasons for fatigue are obvious. You have worked hard and deserve to rest. Plan on an early bedtime for at least a week to help you get over the fatigue. Eat well-balanced meals with 50-60% complex carbohydrates to replenish the body's energy stores. Take in adequate protein to rebuild any tissue damage. Cravings for particular foods should be answered. This may be the body's way of telling you what it needs.

As the stiffness and soreness subside, slowly build up your runs. Think of it as a sort of reverse tapering process. As you dropped hard workouts, then reduced your mileage down to a minimum the day before the marathon, so should you increase your mileage from a minimum the day after, slowly building it until you are ready to do hard workouts again. The maximum should be the same mileage as the week before the marathon. The minimum should be whatever exercise feels good to you. This may be a good time to enjoy a massage from your regular therapist. Several days after the marathon you may feel very strong. This is because your post race lessened activity and eating well have carbohydrate loaded your body! Avoid the temptation to do a hard workout. Unless you are incredibly fit, you have not recovered yet. Stick to your recovery plan.

The Month After the Marathon

If you are not an experienced marathoner, expect to have some long term fatigue during the month following the race. This fatigue usually shows up when you try to do hard or long runs. You will simply "run out of gas". It will go away and eventually you will emerge stronger than ever. As a rule of thumb, allow yourself about 10 training miles for every race mile for a full recovery. When you are back doing regular training and have accumulated 260 training miles, you should be ready to train hard or race again. Now is the time to set some goals for your future racing and make plans for training.

If you are an experienced marathoner with a good training base, these 260 miles of recovery will happen soon. You are in excellent shape, have peaked and may find that you can run some great races. If you plan to race, cut down on your training mileage and recover fully from each one. If you have not fully recovered from the marathon and try to race, you may run excellent times, but you are courting serious injury. Keep setting goals. Plan your training so that you can achieve those goals.

Progressions

Listed below are several post marathon recovery programs. These are only guides. Recovery rates are highly individual and only you can determine whether this program is too short. If soreness or fatigue lingers, back off to the previous week's schedule and give yourself time to heal. If you have persistent pain, you may have injured yourself in the marathon. Try another less stressful aerobic exercise such as bicycling or swimming for a while. If pain is severe, you may need complete rest and the opinion of a physician.

Novice Marathon Recovery

Goal
To recover from the marathon and return to desired training program.

Mileage Progression

Week	S	M	T	W	T	F	S
27	Race	W	W	W	0	2	0
28	4	0	2	4	2	4	0
29	6	0	2	4	2	4	0
30	8	0	2	5	2	5	0

(W) 15-20 minute slow easy walk. Alternative exercise such as swimming or cycling for the same amount of time is another option.

All runs done at an easy, (80% effort), training pace or slower. See easy pace/heart rate charts in appendix.

Beginning Marathon Recovery

Goal
To recover from the marathon and return to desired training program.

Mileage Progression

Week	S	M	T	W	T	F	S
27	Race	W	W	W	0	2	0
28	4	0	2	4	2	4	0
29	8	0	2	4	2	4	0
30	10	0	2	5	2	5	0

(W) 15-20 minute slow easy walk. Alternative exercise such as swimming or cycling for the same amount of time is another option.

All runs done at an easy, (80% effort), training pace or slower. See easy pace/heart rate charts in appendix.

Recreational Marathon Recovery

Goal
To recover from the marathon and return to desired training program.

Mileage Progression

Week	S	M	T	W	T	F	S
27	Race	J/W	J/W	J/W	0	4	0
28	6	0	3	5	3	5	0
29	8	0	3	6	3	6	0
30	12	0	3	7	3	7	0

(J/W) short 15-20 minute jog or walk.

All runs done at an easy, (80% effort), training pace or slower. See easy pace/heart rate charts in appendix.

Intermediate Marathon Recovery

Goal
To recover from the marathon and return to desired training program.

Mileage Progression

Week	S	M	T	W	T	F	S
27	Race	J/W	J/W	3	0	6	4
28	10	0	4	8	4	8	4
29	12	0	4	10	4	8	4
30	16	0	5	10	5	10	5

(J/W) short 15-20 minute jog or walk.

All runs done at an easy, (80% effort), training pace or slower. See easy pace/heart rate charts in appendix.

Advanced Marathon Recovery

Goal
To recover from the marathon and return to desired training program.

Mileage Progressions

Week	S	M	T	W	T	F	S
27	Race	J/W	3	3	5	8	5
28	12	6	6	10	6	10	6
29	16	7	7	12	7	12	7
30	20	7	7	14*	7	14	7

(J/W) short 15-20 minute jog or walk.

* This run optionally can be speed work of 6-7 miles.

All other runs done at an easy, (80% effort), training pace or slower. See easy pace/heart rate charts in appendix.

Aids to Performance

Supplemental Training

By Janet Hamilton

The first step to preventing a running injury is to understand a little of where they come from. There have been numerous studies to figure out why and how runners get injured. All have come up with a fairly consistent picture – there is no *one* reason why runners get injured, but there is a pretty consistent interaction of factors that play a role in runner injuries. Factors commonly recognized include muscle weakness, inadequate flexibility, training errors, poor or abnormal biomechanics, and poor or incorrect running shoes. Each factor has an individual contribution to injury patterns, and can also have an effect on each of the other factors. It can get a little confusing, so it helps to draw a picture to illustrate these interactions.

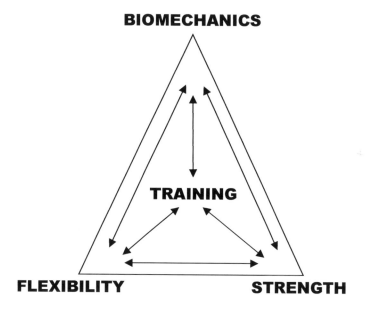

For instance, muscle flexibility can be affected by an individual's biomechanics and likewise, an individual's biomechanics can be affected by their flexibility. A prime example of this is the increase in pronation that takes place as a direct result of loss of flexibility in the calf muscle group. Conversely, people who pronate excessively often have very tight calf muscles. Muscle strength and flexibility also interact with each other. Training errors (like adding too much mileage too fast, or doing too much speedwork) can contribute to microtrauma and a loss of flexibility – leading to a loss of strength and a deterioration of biomechanics. With this picture in mind, it becomes clear that to avoid injury you must deal with as many variables as possible. This next section is devoted to dealing with flexibility, followed by a section dealing with strength training.

Flexibility

Why stretch?
What is the big deal about stretching anyway? You're probably asking yourself "Why should I start now? I've been running for years and never stretched." To put it into perspective, let's look at what your muscles are trying to accomplish when you run and more specifically when you train for an event like a marathon. With each step you take your muscles must contract to absorb the impact forces of your body crashing into the ground and then propel you safely on your way. Let's do the math... if the average stride length is 3.5 feet that amounts to 1175 steps per mile. Now multiply your body weight times 2.5 – that's the amount of impact force being absorbed at *each* foot strike. So, for a 150 pound individual, that totals 440,625 pounds of impact force *per mile*. Now multiply that by a conservative beginners marathon-training schedule of 40 miles per week, you come up with 17,625,000 pounds of impact force per week. Did someone say cumulative trauma? Your muscles must be both flexible and strong to adequately absorb and transform this force into forward momentum. Still not convinced? How about these statistics – Davis reports in "Prevention and Treatment of Running Injuries" that some 92% of injured runners seen in Physical Therapy clinics were found to have inadequate flexibility in one or more muscle groups[3]. Personally I think that statistic is conservative, I'd put it closer to 99%. Plain and simple – if you want to avoid injury the best investment you can make is time spent stretching your muscles. As with all things in life, there's a right and a wrong way to go about things. You need to stretch the right muscle in the correct fashion to reap the benefit. Here's the low down on how to avoid the pitfalls of incorrect stretching.

When to Stretch
Let's set the record straight - if it were dangerous to stretch "cold" every cat and dog in the world would be chronically injured. Now, with that said, it is always more *effective* to stretch a warm muscle and you *DO run a greater risk of injury* when performing *sustained* stretches on cold muscles. With that in mind, the most effective stretching will be done when your muscles are warm, like they are after an easy run, a warm shower or soak in the hot tub. Some researchers put the ideal tissue temperature for stretching at about $39°$ C (or about $102°$ F) [8]. Warmth reduces the viscosity (thickness) of your body fluids, and increases the elasticity of the muscles and connective tissue.

The latest research on flexibility shows that stretching a muscle is a relaxation event that makes the muscle go into a "sleeplike" state. This makes pre run stretching counterproductive. The end of your run or walk is usually the best time to stretch, your muscles are thoroughly warmed up then and ready to be relaxed. Most people find that if they're trying to overcome an injury it helps to take a stretch break part way through their workout. This is especially true as you begin to return to running or walking after an injury. To do this, warm up for a few moments at a slower than usual pace, then stop and stretch the key muscles for about 2 minutes. Then resume your run, starting back at your warm-up pace.

When not to stretch
Sometimes stretching is NOT the thing to do. Generally this is the case immediately following a *severe* muscle strain or sprain where substantial bruising is apparent within 24 hours of injury. In this case, gentle active motion within a *pain free range* is OK, but trying to "stretch it out" may well make the injury worse. Anytime you are performing a stretch and are feeling a pain or pulling sensation in the "wrong" place (i.e. not where you're supposed to be feeling it) you should re-evaluate your position and decide if it is too soon to stretch. Achilles tendonitis is a great example of this. Often in a case of Achilles tendonitis, it is difficult to stretch the calf muscles without feeling the stretch in the Achilles tendon itself. If this is the case, try reducing the intensity of the stretch, and if this reduction in intensity doesn't alleviate the pull in the tendon, then it is too soon to stretch. Stretching immediately after a very long run (more than 15 miles) may not be the best time. Give yourself several minutes to walk to bring your heart rate down to normal and re-hydrate yourself. Walking for at least a half mile after a 10-15 mile run is a great idea. It should be a gentle stroll, and you should be sipping water throughout this cool down. You should do the bulk of your stretching later in the day, after you've rested and had a shower and something to eat. Then take a few moments to warm up by walking around and proceed as usual with your stretches.

How to stretch

There are three basic methods for stretching: static, ballistic, and PNF (proprioceptive neuromuscular facilitation). Ballistic stretching, where you move a body part rhythmically and rapidly into a stretched position, has a high risk for injury and is less than optimal for the type of flexibility you'll need as a marathoner. Those who participate in ballistic type movements as a part of their sport, i.e. Karate, may find it useful after appropriate warm up, and static stretching. However it is the riskiest and least effective form of stretching for runners. PNF stretching is highly effective, but can be difficult to learn just from looking at pictures and reading descriptions. It is best if you're instructed in PNF techniques one-on-one. Each of the three basic methods has their benefits, but we're going to focus on the static stretching method because it has the least risk for injury and is the easiest to accomplish.

Static stretches are usually positions of stretch that are sustained for a period of time, to enable both the contractile and non-contractile elements of the muscle to adapt to the position. That means you need to stretch slowly, moving into position gently and holding the position for about 30 seconds. This will reduce the tendency to stimulate what is called the stretch reflex. The stretch reflex is a protective mechanism that reflexively contracts a muscle if it is rapidly stretched. Sustained stretching will avoid this reflex and allow the muscle to lengthen. A 1994 study in "Physical Therapy" found that the optimum duration of stretch was approximately 30 seconds with no significant benefit to be had from holding it longer [1]. As far as how many repetitions to do of each stretch, a 1990 study in the American Journal of Sports Medicine reported that long lasting increases in flexibility can be achieved with 3-5 repetitions, with little benefit to be had from more repetitions [10].

To perform your stretches correctly, move slowly into the position until you feel a GENTLE "pulling sensation" in the muscle that is being stretched. As you hold this position, breathe and relax – focusing your attention on the muscle that is being stretched. *Avoid the urge to "push it" to the limits.* Simply feel a gentle pull and stay put. Stretching harder will tend to do more harm than good. More is not better in this case! Stretching more frequently throughout the day, or more consistently day after day, will buy you something. Stretching harder will not.

What to Stretch

Every individual is unique, with unique biomechanical, strength, occupational, and training characteristics. However, there are a few muscle groups that are so consistently tight on the majority of runners that it is generally safe for all runners to perform these stretches. Muscles of the calf, hamstrings, hip flexors and quadriceps fall into this category. There are numerous other muscle groups that could benefit from stretching, but this is a good beginning.

A few rules of the road need to be reviewed here, then we'll move on to the specific stretching exercises.

Rules of the Road

1. Pain is <u>never</u> acceptable when stretching. Stretching should be comfortable and relaxing, never painful. If something hurts, you're not in the right position or you've stretched too vigorously. Back off and check your position, then try again more gently.
2. Slow and steady wins the race. Slow movements into the position of stretch will avoid stimulating the stretch reflex, and will allow you to tune into your muscle's signals. Don't rush it. Once in position, hold steady – no bouncing allowed.
3. The position of stretch should generally be held for about 30 seconds.
4. The stretch should occur where indicated on the pictures. If you're feeling it someplace other than there, chances are you're not in the right position. Have a friend look at the picture and then look at you to see if you're in the correct position. There are subtle nuances to the instructions on each of the stretches; attention to these will generally put you in the correct position.
5. Be consistent. The more consistently you perform these stretches the more effective you will be in increasing your flexibility.

Calf Muscle Stretch

Stand with your hands on a wall, and place one foot in front of the other as shown here. Put all your weight on the back foot. *Now for the important part:* **Roll your back foot slightly to the outside to elevate your arch a little (see left figure). Lift your toes a little to lock this position in place (see right figure). Keep your heel down and your knee straight.** Now slightly bend the forward knee, moving your hips toward the wall a little. Make sure to keep your hips right under your shoulders, don't stick your butt out! (Right figure shows the correct shoulder to hip alignment) You should begin to feel a GENTLE stretch or pulling sensation in the calf muscle of the back leg (the one with all the weight on it) - just below your knee. If you feel discomfort in the calf or arch of the foot **BACK OFF!** Don't stretch so hard. Hold this position for about 30 seconds, then switch legs and do the same procedure on the other side.

KEY POINTS

1. All your body weight should be on the back foot
2. Keep your heel down
3. Lift your arch slightly and lock in place by lifting the toes
4. Back leg should have a straight knee
5. Stretch only to the point of a pull - never pain. Hold for at least 30 seconds.

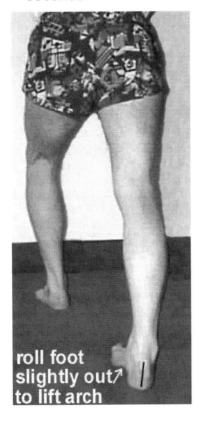
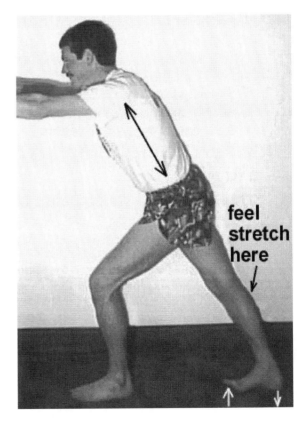

Hamstring Stretch

Form is everything! Stand facing squarely toward a chair and make sure your hips, chest and both feet are all facing directly toward the chair. Without turning your hips, place the heel of one foot up on the chair or low stool - **keeping your knee _slightly_ bent (see arrow).** Now, without fully straightening your knee, try to pull your butt back and chest up at the same time (see arrows). This will put the axis of rotation at your hip joint rather than in your back. Make sure to **_avoid rounding your back._** You should feel a gentle pulling sensation or stretch in the back of the thigh of the leg that is up on the chair. If you feel pain in the back of the thigh or in your lower back region, **BACK OFF!** Don't stretch so hard! If you can't accomplish this position with your foot on a chair, then use a step stool or stack of phone books. Hold the position for a gentle stretch of 30 seconds. Repeat the same procedure on the other side.

KEY POINTS
1. Hips *must* stay square to the chair; turning your hips as you put your foot up on the chair is cheating!
2. Keep the knee slightly bent throughout the stretch.
3. Don't let your back "round" - you must pivot by pulling the butt back and chest up.
4. <u>*Never stretch to the point of pain!*</u> A gentle pull is all it takes.
5. To stretch the upper portion of the hamstrings at their attachment to the hips, bend the knee to about 35 degrees and put more emphasis on pulling the butt back. You should feel the stretch move from the middle of the back of the thigh, to the area where your leg meets your butt.
6. Keep your ankle pulled up (toes pointing toward the ceiling) throughout the stretch.

Hip Flexor Stretch

Start in a half-kneeling position, with one foot flat on the floor and the other knee directly under the hip. You may find it helpful to put a pillow under your knee if the floor is very hard. From this position, check your posture and make sure your back is absolutely straight, with your shoulders, hips and knees all aligned. Since one of the hip flexors attaches to the spine, what you do with your low back affects how well you're able to stretch the hip flexors. Now **perform a pelvic tilt** as shown by the black arrows. To visualize this move, picture yourself "tucking your tail between your legs". If you do this correctly, you'll immediately feel a gentle pull or stretch in the front of the hip and thigh region of the leg you're kneeling on (see white arrows). Breathe, and hold the stretch. If you don't feel any pull *at all* then shift your weight slightly forward, but **keep your pelvic tilt**. If you feel pain anywhere, BACK OFF! Don't stretch so hard! Hold this position for about 30 seconds. Repeat the procedure on the other side.

KEY POINTS

1. Posture is everything here! You **must** maintain your pelvic tilt in order to place the stretch on the hip flexor muscle and avoid placing an undue amount of stress on the lumbar spine.
2. By bending the forward knee and shifting your weight forward, you can increase the stretch, but it is much harder to hold proper pelvic position.

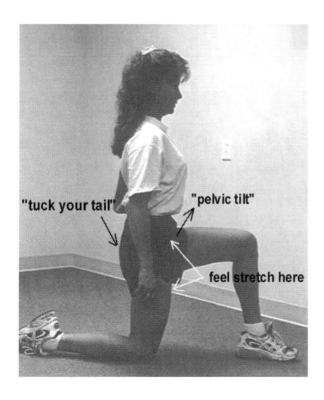

Quadriceps Stretch

Stand next to a wall or chair for balance. Make sure both feet are pointing straight ahead. Loop a towel around one ankle and grasp it with one hand. Pull up on the towel, bringing your heel up slightly toward your buttocks. **Stop when your knee is bent 90 degrees (as in the photo), so you can adjust your posture.** Now, from this position, tighten your stomach muscles as if someone was about to punch you in the gut. This will keep your back from arching. Next, keeping your tummy tight, try to get your knee directly under your hip (see line in photo). Now, *if you don't already feel a stretch in the muscle on the front of your thigh,* pull up slightly on the towel – drawing your heel a little closer to your buttocks (see arrow in photo). You should feel a gentle pull in the muscle of the front of your thigh. If you feel **pain** in your back, or in the front of your thigh, BACK OFF! Don't stretch so hard! Posture is EVERYTHING here! If you lose your tummy muscle control, your back will arch and you'll lose the mechanical advantage to get the optimum stretch on the quad muscle. The goal is not to get the heel to the buttocks, but rather to get the shoulders, hips and knees all in alignment. Hold the stretch for about 30 seconds. Repeat the procedure on the other side.

KEY POINTS

1. Keep your stomach muscles tight throughout this exercise to insure that you aren't arching your back

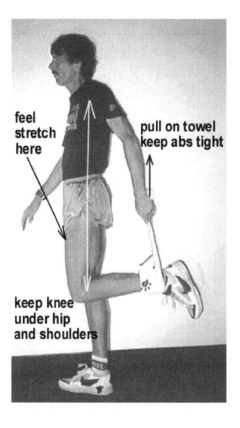

2. The goal is to get the knee directly under the hip, which is directly under the shoulder – *not* to get the foot to the buttocks.
3. Pull on the towel only until you feel a gentle stretch in the front of the thigh, if you feel pain you're stretching too hard.
4. If you are not feeling a stretch using a towel, try grasping the heel counter of your shoe with your index finger – but remember to keep your posture correct.

Strength Training

Why strength train?
Why do I need to focus on strength? Won't running give me the strength I need? Clearly the best shock absorber you have is **not** the one that is laced to your feet – it is your muscular system. Muscles act to resist the gravitational force trying to pull you into the ground every step you take. This gravitational force is roughly equal to 2.5 to 3 times your body weight. Without adequate muscular strength, when your foot hits the ground your knee and hip would collapse and you'd end up in a heap on the pavement. Each time your foot contacts the ground there is a finely orchestrated sequence of muscular contractions that occur to make sure that you land gently and are able to take off again. As your muscles begin to fatigue, your running form suffers and other tissues like tendon and bone are required to absorb a greater portion of the shock incurred. Though these tissues are strong, they're not designed with the same elastic components as muscle and over time they'll be traumatized by the role they're being asked to play. The stronger the muscles, the longer they will take to fatigue and consequently the less risk you have of being injured.

Brute strength isn't the issue here. Remember, depending on your height and stride length, you will take roughly 1175 steps per mile. That means, in a typical marathon, you may do 30,785 repetitions of this "exercise". Thinking of it that way puts the term "endurance exercise" in a whole new light. Fundamentally, your muscles get stronger when you ask them to do some amount of work they are not accustomed to doing. This is what is known as "overload". Overload can take the form of increased intensity (more weight), increased duration (more repetitions), or increased range (more motion). Specificity is the key here. For example, power lifters are training to lift massive amounts of weight for one repetition. In order to be specific, their training takes the form of very high resistance for few repetitions, but moving through a large range of motion. Runners on the other hand need to train for an activity that will be longer in duration, through a relatively smaller range of motion. To maximize the carryover of strength, the training should resemble the activity you're training for as much as possible. For a runner, that means higher repetitions with lower weights.

What is the best method for strength training?

There are dozens of equipment makers that will tell you that their latest model of the "X" machine is the greatest. I am not against using machines, but I find that most of the time they're icing on the cake – not the cake itself. You can do quite well in most cases with body weight, gravity, four walls and a floor. Occasionally it helps to have some hand weights or elastic bands to offer additional resistance. Generally when training for power or strength, using free weights rather than machines is more effective. Using free weights requires that you both lift **and control** the weight. It means that you must contract synergistic muscles to make sure that you accomplish the movement in the right fashion. This way, you train not only the prime movers, but also the muscles that give you controlled, quality movement. A good example is the use of free weights to do a squat, versus using a leg press machine. When doing squats, you must balance the weight appropriately at the start of the exercise and then continuously adjust the balance as your body moves through space and your center of gravity moves. On the other hand when you sit in a leg press machine (or lie on the inverted style ones), you don't have to balance a thing – just push against the machine and it will maintain the proper alignment because it is designed to do just that. You may gain strength from this exercise, but you'll not gain the same amount of control, balance and power as you would if you spent the same amount of time doing a free weight exercise like a squat. With that said, it is sometimes *better* to use machines for strength training. Instances where this comes to mind include individuals who have a compromised sense of balance, and individuals who are recovering from a traumatic injury and must avoid certain motions or firing certain muscles. Generally even if you've never lifted weights before, you can learn to perform free-weight exercises. After all, your body is a free weight and you seem to handle it pretty well, don't you?

When to train

There is no one "best" time of day to strength train. Work it into your schedule as it suits you. There are however, cycles of training that can prove beneficial. Think of the professional sports teams – they have an off season as well as a competitive season. The majority of the strength building is done in the off season; skill building and other things are emphasized as the competitive season approaches. Following this same theory, runners would do well to cycle their training somewhat. Pick a couple of events in which you'd like to do well. Then cycle your training so that you have a rest season right after a racing season, and a period of strength and base building before the racing season, and a segment devoted to speed building as the racing season nears. The choice of when during the training week to do your strength training is very individual. Some like to do their strength training workouts on their "easy" mileage days, others like to do it on the "medium" mileage days. Experiment and do what ever works best for you. I would *not* recommend you do your strength-training workout on a long mileage day or on a day in which you will be doing speedwork.

Reps, sets, and such

A "rep" is one repetition of a motion – one squat, one lunge, one bench press. A "set" is a group of repetitions of an exercise – one set of 10 repetitions, one set of 15 repetitions, etc. Multiple sets are often done. These are generally separated by a rest break. For example, to do 3 sets of 15 reps of squats, you would perform the first set of 15 reps and then rest for a brief period (60 seconds or so) before doing the second set, likewise rest before the third set. Generally the more endurance you're trying to build, the more repetitions you'll be doing. Runners will benefit from doing sets of 20-30 repetitions of an exercise.

Increasing the intensity

There are a myriad of ways to make an exercise harder – depending on the exercise and the equipment you're using (if any). If you're using free weights or machines, it is best to increase the resistance by the smallest possible increment. In some cases this may be a 10 pound increase, in others it may be as little as 2-3 pounds. Regardless, you want to make the changes gradual. Increase the resistance only when you can accomplish the specified reps and sets of the exercise and feel only minimally taxed at the end. If you're struggling *at all* with the current weight, don't increase it. Increasing the resistance each workout is a very bad idea and will surely put you at greater risk of injury. Give yourself at least 4-6 workouts at a specified resistance before even thinking about increasing it. For exercises done with body weight only, sometimes increasing the range of motion will be enough to make the exercise harder. For example, if you've been doing one-quarter depth squats, try squatting to chair height (half-depth). If you've been doing balance and reach exercises, reach farther. If you've been doing lunges, lunge a little deeper or take a bigger step. Sometimes simply doing a balance and reach exercise with your eyes closed is a good way to challenge yourself. This puts a whole new meaning to the concept of balance.

What will I feel the next day?

Generally, strength training will give most people at least some "delayed onset muscle soreness". This occurs in most people within 48 hours of performing the strength-training workout. This is one good reason to **start slowly – do less than you think you can the first few workouts.** You'll be surprised at just how little it takes of some exercises to bring on the soreness, so proceed with caution. The delayed onset soreness is a result of micro-trauma to the muscles and indicates that you probably pushed your limits a bit. Generally this soreness can be classified as follows:

- "Acceptable" - a little sore with some movements (like getting up/down from toilet, in/out of car etc.) but just walking around isn't painful.
- "Pushing it" - noticeably sore with most movements, including just walking around.
- "Overdoing it" - lying in bed and turning over hurts.

Generally if you can keep your soreness at the acceptable level or less, and you're not feeling any joint pain, you're doing OK. If you're feeling more pain in the joints than the muscles, or if you're "pushing it" or "overdoing it" – you need to back off and take several days rest before trying again. Strength training stimulates muscles to get stronger by pushing them to their limits. If you consistently push beyond those limits, you run the risk of causing an injury. Try not to get into the "No pain, No gain" syndrome.

When in doubt...
Listen to your body, pain is the universal signal that something is wrong. If you're having pain in your joints, either the exercise is too advanced for you or you're increasing the intensity too fast, or your form is off. If you're new to strength training, start slowly and focus on technique first.

What to strengthen
Muscles most involved in absorbing ground reaction forces during running are the quadriceps, hamstrings, and gluteal muscles. These are the obvious ones; however, there are a whole host of other muscles in your body that also need to work. Included are the muscles involved in the core of the body, the abdominal muscles and the muscles in your back. These postural muscles may not be as obvious, but they're vital. As you fatigue on a long run, you'll have a tendency to pull your shoulders up toward your ears in an attempt to overcome the forces of gravity. Likewise, you'll have a tendency to let your upper body sag, decreasing the space available in your chest. To prove this point, sit or stand with very erect posture and take a deep breath. Now slouch and try to take a deep breath. It is nearly impossible to get the same amount of air in your lungs if your rib cage is squashing them. To avoid this scenario, strengthen the core muscles as well as the leg muscles. Let's start with the core muscles – the abdominal and spinal muscles.

Crunches

This exercise is to strengthen the abdominal muscles. To protect your back and to place the greatest demand on your abdominal muscles, place your feet up on a chair or bench. You can rest your calves on the bench as well. Now, **without pulling your chin to your chest,** contract your abdominal muscles and lift your head and shoulders slightly off the floor. Hold this position for 3 seconds, then lower your body back to the start position. To work your oblique abdominal muscles, reach both of your hands to the right of the right leg and then to the left of the left leg. Alternate directions each repetition. To make the exercise more difficult, fold your arms across your chest, or place them behind your head – *but make sure to keep the proper head alignment.* Pulling your chin to your chest will strain your neck. If you have discomfort in your lower back, try adjusting your position slightly – placing more of your leg on the bench, and don't lift your body so far off the floor. **Small lifts** will isolate the abdominal muscles without putting strain on the lower back. Start out with 10-15 repetitions in each of the three directions (diagonal right, straight, diagonal left) and progressively add repetitions until you can do a set of 20-30 repetitions. At this point, you're ready to add a second set, but don't forget to rest between sets.

KEY POINTS
1. Use the abdominal muscles to lift your head and shoulders slightly off the floor, don't pull with your neck muscles.
2. If you put your hands across your chest or behind your head,

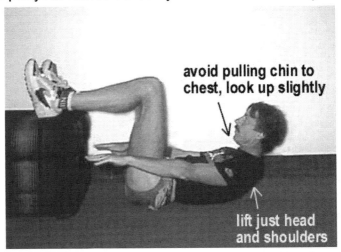

don't forget to keep your chin up. It helps to "spot" a place on the ceiling and try to focus on it. Alternating directions, lifting to the right, then center, then left – will effectively reach not only the front of the abdominal muscles but also the oblique abdominal muscles.

3. You should never feel pain in your lower back or neck with this exercise. The only place you should feel fatigue is the abdominal muscles. If you're having pain, then your form is incorrect, or you're trying to lift your body too far off the floor. Back off, check your form and try again.

Prone opposite arm and leg extension

This exercise is designed to strengthen all the muscles of your back from your upper back all the way down to your lower back. To do this exercise, start by lying on the floor on your stomach with your arms and legs stretched out straight. Both arms should be straight overhead and your forehead and chin should be resting on the floor. **Do not** turn your head to the side. Lift the right arm and left leg off the floor, while being sure to keep them straight. The focus is **not** on getting them high in the air; it is on **_lengthening_** your body by attempting to maximize the distance between your toes and your fingertips. Lifting your arm or leg too high will place a strain on your lower back, so avoid this tendency and **focus on making your body as long as possible.** If you find that you have a hard time with lifting both the arm and leg simultaneously, you can lift one extremity at a time, lifting first one leg then another and then lifting the arms one at a time. As you gain strength you can progress to lifting diagonal pairs. Hold the position for about 3-5 seconds, then lower the arm and leg and repeat the lift with the opposite diagonal pair. Repeat this series until you've done 15 repetitions on each side. Add repetitions as you get stronger, until you can do a set of 20-30 repetitions. At this point you're ready to add a second set. Remember that you should rest between sets for about a minute or two. You should feel the muscles in your back working, but it should NOT be painful. You may well have a little muscle soreness the next day, but this should gradually resolve as you gain strength. Avoid the urge to add repetitions every day, and don't increase the reps or sets until you can accomplish the previous level with no soreness the next day.

KEY POINTS
1. Focus on lengthening the body, not trying to lift the arm and leg high in the air.
2. Make sure to keep your head straight, don't turn it to the side. If you have discomfort in your lower back, you're probably lifting too high or you're just not strong enough to lift both the leg and arm at the same time. Try decreasing the height of your lift, or switch to just lifting one extremity at a time.

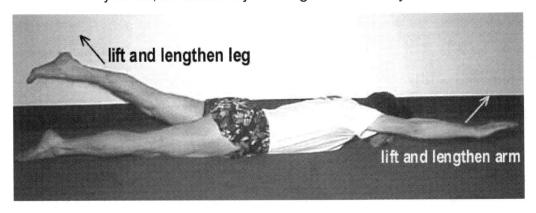

3. You may experience a little muscle soreness in your back the next day when you first start doing these exercises. Don't progress your repetitions until you can accomplish the exercise with minimal difficulty and no soreness in your muscles the next day.

Squats

Probably the most functional exercise you'll ever learn, the squat is a basic fundamental movement that you repeat numerous times throughout the day. Every time you sit in a chair, you performed a squat to get there. Every time you get up, you get up from a squat. This exercise is the basis for safe lifting mechanics as well. Utilizing the body mechanics shown in the photo, you keep your back in a position of safety and use the large muscles of your buttocks and thighs to accomplish the task at hand. Start this exercise standing with your feet a shoulder's width apart. Your toes should be pointing ahead or very slightly turned out. Place your hands on your hips, to remind you that you're to pivot from the hips not the back. Now, **keeping your back straight but _NOT vertical_**, squat down as if you were going to sit on a chair but you didn't know how low it was. As you squat, your chest should be over your knees, which are over your feet – making your center of gravity very stable and centered over your feet. If you feel yourself falling backwards, you're not pivoting from the hips –

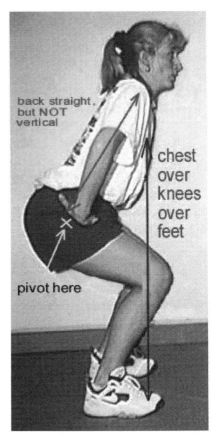

bring your chest more over your knees. You should be able to squat to chair height **without lifting your heels** off the ground. Sometimes it helps to think "butt back" and "chest over knees" as you do this movement. As you get the hang of it, try folding your arms across your chest, or placing your hands clasped behind your neck. This will change your center of gravity slightly and force you to pivot from the hips. It helps to do this exercise in front of a full-length mirror to check your form, or have a partner look at this picture and check your form. **FORM is everything** on this one. How low you squat depends on how well you can maintain form, your ankle flexibility, the condition of your knee joints and several other factors. Depth is not the issue here, _form is_. Squat only to a depth that is comfortable for you. You should be able to maintain good form throughout the movement. If you're unsure of yourself, place a chair behind you and squat until your buttocks just barely brush the edge of the chair seat. This will give you a "target" to aim for. Don't hold the position, just squat down and then return to the starting position. If you feel pain anywhere don't squat so low! Try to perform 10-15 repetitions of this exercise and gradually build up to 20-30 repetitions before adding a second set. This is a great warm up exercise for the other leg strengthening exercises that will follow.

KEY POINTS
1. Feet should be a shoulder width apart, toes facing straight ahead or very slightly toed out.
2. Keep your back straight but not vertical, it helps to think "stick your butt back" and "keep your chest over your knees".
3. Keep both heels on the ground, this makes sure that your base of support is stable and encourages you to pivot from the hips.
4. Squat only as deep as you can go without losing your good form. Most people can eventually squat to chair seat height with good form. Some can eventually maintain good form even deeper than that.
5. Depth is not the issue – form is.
6. If you feel pain in your knee joints, don't squat so low – keep the movement pain free. You should feel your thigh muscles and buttock muscles working, but you should not have joint pain anywhere. If you're having back pain, your form is incorrect – squat to a shallower depth and work on keeping your back straight and chest over knees.
7. To increase the intensity of the exercise, try holding a broomstick across your shoulders, behind your head. Another way to make it more difficult is to hold small hand weight, or use a light barbell in place of the broomstick. Varying the speed of the squat - sometimes going faster or slower will also change the intensity of the exercise. Obviously, squatting deeper also makes it more intense – but you've got to maintain form.

Lateral lunges

This exercise focuses on the inner and outer thigh muscles. These muscles play a major role in controlling pronation and stabilizing your hips and pelvis. Start from a standing position, with your feet together and facing straight ahead. Take a big step to the side with one foot, and as your weight shifts onto that foot, bend your knee and lunge to the side. Make sure to keep your shoulders and hips parallel and facing squarely ahead. The leg that is stationary (back at home base) should remain **straight**, not flexing at the knee. Don't hold this position, simply lunge and then push off to return to the starting position. Take as large a step as you are able to, making sure that you're able to return to the starting position with one push. Multiple hops to return to the start position means you took too large a step. How deep you lunge is not important and will depend in part on your muscle

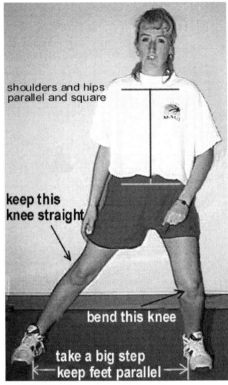

strength, the condition of your knee joints, flexibility in your ankles, and your sense of balance. **Depth is not the issue here, form is.** Make sure to maintain good posture throughout the exercise, and <u>keep your feet parallel</u> to each other and facing straight ahead at all times. Avoid the urge to toe out on the lunging leg. To work on stamina, do all the repetitions on one leg before you switch and repeat the process on the other side. If you feel any pain in your knee joints or anywhere else, BACK OFF! Don't step so far or lunge so deep! The exercise should always be pain free. You may feel the muscles in your hips and thighs working but it should never be painful. Start out with a set of 10-15 repetitions on each side and gradually build up to a set of 20-30 repetitions before adding a second set.

KEY POINTS
1. Make sure your feet are parallel at all times and facing straight ahead.
2. Take as big a step as you can, but make sure you're able to get back to the starting position with just one push. If you have to hop back to the start position, you took too big a step.
3. Keep your shoulders and hips level and squarely facing forward.

4. To increase the intensity of the exercise, try holding a broomstick on your shoulders behind your head or hold some light hand weights in your hands. Stepping further and lunging deeper also make this exercise more intense, but make sure that you're not losing your good form or causing any discomfort when you do this. Also doing this exercise with your eyes closed, or varying the speed will change the dynamics.
5. Remember, the exercise is to be pain free, if you're having discomfort anywhere – check your form. Shorter steps and shallower depths usually take care of the problem. You should feel the muscles in your hips and thighs working, but you shouldn't feel any pain.

Balance and backward diagonal reach
Perhaps the quintessential strengthening exercise, the balance and reach exercise challenges the prime muscles as well as their synergistic partners and offers a challenge to the proprioceptive system as well. This intricate system is made up of receptors in your muscles, tendons and joints that coordinate their input with input from your inner ear and your visual system. To say it is complex is an understatement. This finely coordinated feedback system is largely responsible for keeping you upright and allowing you to recover your balance when you lose it. The biggest benefit of using a balance and reach style of exercise to strengthen your muscles is that it simultaneously provides stimulus to the proprioceptive system that you wouldn't get if you were sitting on a machine and performing a similar strength training exercise.

This particular variation of the balance and reach exercise works your hip and thigh muscles. Like all balance and reach exercises the rules are simple: you balance on one leg and then reach but don't touch. By holding your balance on one leg while you dynamically move your other leg, you challenge your body's intricate balance system at the same time you're challenging your muscles to get stronger. You get a lot of bang for the buck here.

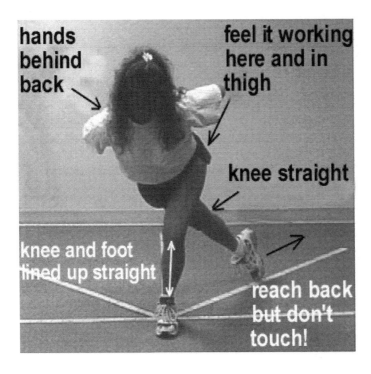

Start by standing straight, with your arms tucked behind your back like a speed skater. Make sure both feet are facing straight ahead. Now, balance on your left leg and reach your right back and diagonally to your left. ***Try to keep your foot within one inch of the floor, but don't touch - that's cheating.*** Reach as far back along that line as you can, stretching your knee straight to maximize the reach. Make sure to keep your left knee lined up over your foot, don't let it fall to the inside. Don't hold the position, just reach and then return to the start position and then repeat. To stimulate more stamina, do all your reps on one leg before switching and repeating the process on the other side. Reach only as far as you're able to go without touching your foot down to the floor for balance. You should never feel pain with this exercise; though you may well feel the muscles of your buttocks and legs working very hard. If you feel pain in the knees, back or anywhere else, BACK OFF! Don't reach so far. Start out with a set of 10-15 repetitions and gradually build up to a set of 20-30 repetitions before adding a second set. This exercise can be pretty intense, so don't rush to add repetitions too soon.

KEY POINTS
1. For maximum challenge keep your hands behind your back, and don't touch your foot to the floor. If you're having trouble with your balance though, it's OK to cheat for awhile until you get stronger. If you're really having trouble, you can hold the wall for balance or use a chair back for support – but the goal is to eventually do it with no assistance.
2. Keep your back straight throughout the movement, pivot from the hip rather than the spine.
3. The farther you reach, the more challenging the exercise; reach as far as you can without pain or losing your balance.

REFERENCES
1. Bandy WD, Irion JM: The effect of time on static stretch on the flexibility of the hamstring muscles. Physical Therapy 74:845-850, 1994.
2. Brooks GA, Fahey TD: Exercise Physiology Human Bioenergetics and Its Applications. New York, Macmillan Publishing Co., 1985.
3. D'Ambrosia RD, Drez D (eds): Prevention and Treatment of Running Injuries, 2nd Edition. Thorofare, NJ, Slack, 1989.
4. Donatelli, RA (ed): The Biomechanics of the Foot and Ankle. 2nd Edition. Philadelphia, FA Davis, 1996.
5. Guten, Gary N (ed): Running Injuries. Philadelphia, WB Saunders Company, 1997.
6. Gould, James A. III (ed): Orthopedic and Sports Physical Therapy. 2nd Edition. St. Louis, CV Mosby, 1990.
7. Gray, Gary W: Lower Extremity Functional Profile. Adrian MI, Wynn Marketing, 1995.
8. Malone TR, Garrett WE Jr., Zachazewski JE: Muscle: Deformation, injury, repair. In Zachazewski JE, Magee DJ, Quillen WS (eds): Athletic Injusryies and Rehabilitation. WB Saunders, Philadelphia, 1996.
9. Root ML, Orien WP, Weed JH: Normal and Abnormal Function of the Foot. Los Angeles, Clinical Biomechanics Corporation, 1977.
10. Taylor DC, Dalton JD Jr, Seaber AV, Garrett WE Jr: Viscoelastic properties of muscle-tendon units: The biomechanical effects of stretching. American Journal of Sports Medicine 18:300-309, 1990.

Food and Performance

As you discovered in the physiology section, the sources of energy for running come from the breakdown of the food you eat. Proper intake of food or good nutrition is important for you to optimize training of the energy systems. The focus of sports nutrition includes maintaining hydration, fueling performance and promoting rapid recovery.

Human nutrition is thought to require six general classes of nutrients. These are carbohydrates, fats, protein, vitamins, minerals and water. These nutrients are essential for human life and inadequate intake may result in disturbed body metabolism, disease or death. Not all necessary nutrients are contained in any one food and an intake of what is called "a balanced diet" is necessary to achieve adequate nutrition.

Food has three major functions. The first is to provide energy for human metabolism. Carbohydrates and fats are the prime sources of energy. Protein can also provide energy, but that is not its major function. The second function of food is to build and repair body tissues. Protein is the major building material for muscles and other soft tissues while minerals such as calcium and phosphorus are used to build and repair bony tissue. Regulation of body processes is the third function of food. Vitamins, minerals and proteins work together to perform this function. These three functions become increasingly more important to the physically active person. Metabolic activities may increase by tenfold for long periods. Physical performance may be hampered seriously by inadequate nutrition. On the other hand, studies on supplemental feeding beyond adequate intake have not revealed an increased capacity for physical performance. The key is to be certain that you are receiving optimal amounts of each specific nutrient. Getting that adequate nutrition during hard training can be a real challenge for athletes. Many athletes have a tendency to underfuel themselves especially those worrying about weight control. Underfueling can lead to sluggishness, fatigue, poor performance, injury and even permanent alteration (lowering) of basal metabolism. Athletes need fuel to perform. We suggest that if you are having problems getting adequate nutrition, it may be helpful to visit a sports dietician to get a dietary plan that works for you.

How Much to Eat

You can roughly estimate your daily caloric requirements by knowing your BMR (basal metabolic rate or the calories needed by your body for basic existence) plus the calories burned by your training and other activities during the day. You can estimate your BMR calories by multiplying your body weight by 10. For example, a 150 lb person would have an estimated BMR of 1500 calories. An athlete with a long history of dieting or reduced calorie consumption should subtract 300 - 500 calories from the BMR calculation. Typical daily activity adds somewhere between 300 and 1000 calories per day. If you have a desk job and are fairly sedentary, add 300 calories; add up to 1,000 calories if your job demands physical labor and you're on your feet all day. Each mile of running consumes about 100 calories. Caloric needs per mile are more dependent on your body weight rather than how fast you run. The food that the athlete eats provides energy and replaces the calories burned. A look at the caloric needs of two marathoners gives you an idea of the caloric needs of training. A 120 pound female with a desk job running 40 miles per week need about 2100 calories per day while her 180 pound male counterpart training the same amount should be eating 2700 calories daily.

What Nutrients to Eat

The runner, just like every one else, should be eating a healthy well balanced diet with 60-65% of the calories being derived from carbohydrates (CHO). About 12-15% of your diet should be protein; leaving about 20-25% to come from fats. You have to have a well balanced diet as well as adequate calories to have adequate nutrition.

Carbohydrates

Carbohydrates (CHO's) are formed when the energy of the sun is harnessed in plants. Simple CHO's are sugars while complex CHO's are many sugars bonded together, known as starches. These are mainly found in plants, as is cellulose, a fiber that does not break down in the presence of human digestive enzymes. Cellulose or fiber adds bulk to the diet to prevent constipation and other problems of the large intestine.

Complex carbohydrates are found mainly in the bread-cereal group and the fruit-vegetable group. Foods such as dry beans, dry peas, milk and ice cream also contain CHO's. Complex rather than simple carbohydrates should be stressed. A study from the E. B. Smith Performance Lab at Texas A&M University showed that of runners who were consuming 25, 50 or 70% carbohydrate diets, only the 70% diet could bring their muscle glycogen back to their pre-exercise level. Other exercise physiologists agree that the high consumption of complex carbohydrates is essential for the endurance athlete, but disagree on the exact levels.

Carbohydrates can be characterized by their speed of conversion to blood glucose. This speed is called glycemic index with classifications of high, moderate and low with high being the fastest. The index is regulated by a number of factors besides whether the CHO is simple or complex. Examples of high glycemic index foods are glucose, sucrose, maltodextrin, syrup, breads, raisins, and potatoes. Moderate glycemic index foods include rice, oatmeal, spaghetti, grapes, oranges and yams. Fruits, fructose, legumes and dairy products have low glycemic indexes. It does not appear that the rate of conversion is different for liquids or solids.

Complex CHO's are broken down into simple sugars (glucose and fructose) and absorbed into the blood. Glucose is blood sugar. It may be transported either to liver or muscle and stored as glycogen. Liver glycogen can later be converted to blood glucose. The greatest amount of CHO is stored in the body as muscle glycogen. Excess blood glucose may be stored as fat or may be excreted. It is possible for the body to make blood glucose by liver action from protein and fat, but this metabolism is inefficient and potentially dangerous.

Glucose is the major supplier of energy for the body especially for the brain and muscles. Muscle glycogen in the active muscles is the primary CHO source for energy. As the muscle glycogen is used, blood glucose enters the muscles to maintain muscle glycogen stores and the liver releases some of its glucose to maintain blood sugar levels.

Muscle glycogen stores can be increased through training and by using the technique of carbohydrate loading. CHO loading is useful for the marathon and requires an increase in carbohydrate content of the diet. Carbohydrate loading is covered under Race Preparation. There you will learn the best method for loading.

Fats
Fats or lipids is the general term for a number of different compounds found in the body in the form of solid fat or liquid oil. Triglycerides are the primary form in which fats are eaten and stored in the human body. They are composed of fatty acids (FA) attached to a glycerol molecule. The difference between saturated and unsaturated fatty acids concerns the chemical degree of hydrogen saturation of the chemical chain of carbon and hydrogen. Practically speaking, saturated fats are usually solid and are derived from animals, while unsaturated fats are liquid and are derived from vegetables. Fat content in foods can vary from 100% in cooking oils to less than 5-10% in vegetables. There are three uses for dietary fat; meet energy needs, provide essential fatty acids and provide essential fat soluble vitamins. Sufficient amounts of fat are found in the average diet; in fact, the problem is usually to refrain from ingesting excessive amounts of fat. Evidence shows dietary fat is more readily stored as body fat than other nutrients.

Fats are a concentrated energy supply for the body providing 9 calories for every gram making them an easy way to add excess calories to the diet. Fats are used in the diet to make foods taste better by providing flavor, aroma and texture. They satisfy the appetite and delay the return of hunger because they take longer to leave the stomach and be digested. They also dilute the nutrient value of foods by increasing calories without increasing nutrients.

Cholesterol is a fat-like pearly substance called a sterol that is found in animal products. In the human body, cholesterol is manufactured from FA's and the breakdown of CHO and protein. Cholesterol is used in the formation of several hormones and is a component of several tissues. It is vital to human physiology, but since it is manufactured in the body, there is little apparent need to obtain it through food. A relationship has been found between high blood cholesterol levels and coronary heart disease (CHD).

Fats are digested mainly in the small intestine recombining into fat droplets in the bloodstream. If you are well fed, the majority of the fat is deposited in the adipose or fat tissue of the body and converted back into triglycerides. The adipose tissue is the body's major energy storage depot and acts as an insulator and shock absorber for various organs. If you are in a fasting state, fat enters the muscle cells where it is either used immediately or stored for future energy use. Your energy balance determines whether fat stores increase or decrease. Excess carbohydrates and proteins are converted by the body to fat and stored in the adipose tissue when food intake is greater than energy output.

The liver regulates the blood lipid level. The lipids in the blood do not circulate as free compounds, but are bound to a protein complex and are known as lipoproteins. These lipoproteins can be grouped into three classes:

VLDL: very low-density lipoproteins - transport triglycerides to the tissues and then become LDL.

LDL: low density lipoproteins - contain a high proportion of cholesterol and supply this to cells needing it. LDL may be taken up by the cells of the artery walls leading to plaque formation and is implicated in the development of atherosclerosis. "Bad Cholesterol"

HDL: high density lipoproteins - contain a high proportion of protein and moderate amounts of cholesterol. HDLs remove cholesterol from the artery walls and return it to the liver for degradation. HDL associated with lower incidence of coronary heart disease. "Good Cholesterol"

Coronary heart disease is atherosclerosis or plaque formation in the coronary blood vessels that narrows them and reduces blood flow to the heart. A number of risk factors have been found for heart disease. These include improper diet, high serum lipids, high serum cholesterol, physical inactivity, obesity, high blood pressure, smoking, age, heredity, and sex (being male). Dietary modifications have been shown to lower serum cholesterol and triglycerides. These modifications include adjusting caloric intake to maintain ideal body weight, reducing simple sugars and alcohol in the diet and increasing complex CHO's, decreasing dietary cholesterol, and reducing the total amounts of fat in the diet especially animal fats. Diets rich in saturated fat tend to raise serum cholesterol while polyunsaturated fats tend to lower it. Exercise has been shown to increase HDL that may contribute to protection against coronary heart disease. High fat diets have also been implicated in increased risk of breast and colon cancers. Increasing flavanols (bioactive compounds found in fruits, vegetables, tea, red wine and dark chocolate) in your diet has been shown to inhibit oxidation of LDL cholesterol and reduce risk of CHD, stoke and hypertension. The flavanols tend to provide more health benefits than performance benefits.

Digested fats are transported to adipose tissue storage sites and to muscle to be stored as triglycerides. Fatty acids for energy production can come from the blood stream or from local stores within the muscle. In prolonged mild to moderate exercise, the fat energy stores come mainly from the muscles and from the blood free fatty acids (FFA's). Utilization of fat from the adipose stores requires ezymes to mobilize the fat and enymes to break it into the FFA's. Fat can supply the majority of energy as long as the exercise remains mild to moderate. As you run faster, the FFA release from adipose tissue slows and the muscle cell begins to rely more and more on CHO as the major energy source. The muscle stores of triglyceride become increasingly important in endurance events. Specific endurance training helps you to increase the muscle triglyceride utilization, burning more fat at faster paces and sparing muscle glycogen. In fact, increased utilization of fat during exercise is a major effect of endurance training.

A physically active person does not need to increase fat intake. Even the leanest runners have adequate fat stores to use as energy and the body can also manufacture fat from carbohydrate and protein. Optimally for runners training heavily, fats should comprise less than 25% of the diet to allow consumption of adequate carbohydrates.

Protein

Carbon, hydrogen, oxygen and nitrogen combine to form structures called amino acids. These amino acids are then combined to form the proteins necessary for the structure and functions of the body. The body can form some of the amino acids that are termed nonessential. Those that it cannot are called essential amino acids and must be obtained from the foods in your diet.

The protein found in animal products contains all of the essential amino acids and, therefore, is called complete protein. These amino acids are also contained in the proper proportions necessary for synthesizing proteins within the body. Protein is found in lesser amounts in plant materials but may be lower in three essential amino acids. Vegetables such as legumes and grains can be combined to create a complete supply of essential amino acids. Soy proteins provide almost as complete a source of protein as animal foods.

Protein is found in every cell in the body. It has many functions such as the formation of new tissues and the replacement of worn out ones. It also regulates the balance of water, the balance of acids and bases and transports nutrients in and out of cells. Protein forms antibodies, hormones and enzymes. Protein transports nutrients and oxygen in the blood and is essential for blood clotting.

The amount of protein necessary in the diet varies with different life stages with the growth phase requiring the most. The need stabilizes in early adulthood. Throughout the life cycle the protein requirement is based on the weight of the individual. The body needs a new supply of protein every day since excess protein is stored not as amino acids but as fat. Excess intake of protein can lead to increased fat stores and can strain the kidneys in an effort to rid the body of it.

Protein is not a major energy source, but excess protein may be converted to carbohydrate or fat. The demand for energy in the body takes precedence over tissue building. During periods of starvation or semi-starvation when adequate amounts of fat and CHO are not available, protein can be utilized for energy. The active individual who desires to maintain lean body mass must have adequate fat and CHO calories to spare protein to be used for its more important functions. The diet of 15 % protein allows for adequate intake. Many of the common sources of protein are high in fat and calories. Go lean with protein. Look for animal protein with less fat such as low fat dairy products, poultry and fish. Combine small amounts of animal protein with plant sources.

Protein intake before exercise has been shown to decrease muscle damage and enhance recovery. During exercise, protein usually contributes only 1-2% of the energy. Recent research has shown that protein may contribute about 4% of energy demand during prolonged exercise with normal glycogen stores. The percentage may rise to 10% if you are depleted of glycogen, as in the last part of the marathon. CHO loading may have a protein sparing effect for distance runners. There are some data to support the recommendations to increase protein intake during endurance training. The current daily recommendation for endurance athletes is 0.6 to 0.9 g/lb of body weight. The overall results show that prolonged low protein intake may have adverse effects on physical performance, but intakes above what is considered normal have not been shown to improve performance.

Vitamins
Vitamins are extremely complex organic compounds found in small amounts in food. They are essential to the optimal functioning of the physiological processes of the human body. Since these processes increase greatly during exercise, an adequate supply of vitamins must be available. Vitamins are essential in human nutrition because of their role in the formation of body enzymes. These enzymes deteriorate over time necessitating a constant fresh supply of vitamins.

Vitamins are not a source of energy and do not have caloric value. They do not contribute to body structure. They are, however, indispensable for regulating body function, or maintenance of optimal health and for optimal athletic performance. No scientific evidence proves that extra vitamins will increase either strength or endurance, provide energy or build muscle.

Vitamins are divided into 2 classes, fat-soluble and water-soluble. Fat-soluble vitamins include Vitamins A, D, E and K. Some essential water-soluble vitamins are Vitamins B1, B2, Niacin, B6, Pantothenic Acid, Folacin, B12, Biotin, Choline, Inositol, and C. Fat-soluble vitamins are stored in the body to a greater degree than water-soluble vitamins. Most vitamins must be obtained from food. A few are formed within the body.

The only difference between natural and synthetic vitamins is the way they are made. Usually it is better to get vitamins from food because they are in combination with minerals and other nutrients needed by the body. Synthetic vitamins may be indicated when deficiencies are noted. Most dieticians feel that there is no evidence that the average American on a balanced diet suffers from vitamin deficiency. Little evidence exists to support the use of vitamin supplements by well-nourished athletes or other highly active persons. If you feel that you are not receiving a balanced diet for any reason, reasonable doses of vitamin supplements (1 mutlivitamin per day) will not be harmful. However, excess quantities or megadoses can have undesirable side effects and are dangerous. A registered dietitian can answer more detailed questions regarding vitamin intake.

Minerals
A mineral is a solid inorganic element found in nature. Twenty-five of the elements are essential in humans and have a wide variety of functions. Some are used as building blocks for body tissues while others are important components of enzymes and hormones. Others regulate the physiologic processes of the body. Some major minerals are calcium, phosphorus, sodium, potassium, chloride, magnesium and iron.

Inadequate intake of calcium by adults can result in a loss of bone density and in muscle cramps. Many experts believe that an adequate intake of calcium is between 1000 and 1500 milligrams per day. Good sources of dietary calcium are low fat dairy products, soy milk, dried beans and many vegetables; especially green leafy ones. Calcium needs Vitamin D to be absorbed which should pose no problems to those who run outdoors most days.

Iron is important for the transport and utilization of oxygen. Iron deficiency is sometimes found in women of child bearing age, vegetarians and endurance athletes who ingest little animal-based protein. Heme iron from beef is the most readily absorbed form of iron leading dieticians to add 1-3 servings of lean beef per week to the runners diet. Better iron absorption from the dietary sources of meat, poultry and fish is obtained when these are combined with Vitamin C rich fruit or vegetables. Vegetarians need to include plant foods with high iron content.

Sodium and chloride combine to form common table salt. Excess salt consumption has been linked to hypertension in certain individuals. The average American consumes about 2-4 teaspoons of salt per day. The suggested daily allotment, far in excess of actual need, is set at between 1-2 teaspoons per day. Enough sodium is naturally present in foods to meet the daily requirements of everyone with the possible exception of those who exercise strenuously in hot weather. If you are running in the heat, you should not restrict your salt intake unless advised to do so by your physician.

A potassium rich diet may guard against hypertension and may control blood pressure. Potassium is important in the conduction of nerve impulses and for the proper functioning of muscle tissue including the formation of muscle glycogen. Potassium is lost through sweat. Low levels will produce muscle weakness and fatigue. It is essential to have adequate supplies in the daily diet especially for those who sweat heavily.

Water
Water, the most important nutrient, is a compound composed of 2 parts hydrogen and one part oxygen. Water provides no food energy or calories, but is needed by every cell to carry out essential functions.

About two thirds of the body weight is water with the majority being within the cells. Water is the main transport mechanism within the body for carrying oxygen, nutrients and hormones to the cells and removing waste products. The waste products are eliminated from the body through the water in sweat, urine and feces. Water also regulates osmotic pressure controlling the proper electrolyte balance and acid/base balance. Water lubricates and cushions. It acts as the body's main cooling system.

The requirement for water depends on the weight and age of the individual, but the average adult needs about 2-3 quarts of water a day to maintain water balance within the body. The balance is maintained when intake of water matches output of body fluids. The main output for water is urine, however, some is lost in the feces and some through exhaled air. Insensible perspiration, which cannot be seen, is a significant source of body water loss. Sweat losses increase greatly with exercise or hot environmental conditions.

The major source of water is fluid intake. Solid foods also contribute through their water content and through metabolism of these foods for energy. Fat, CHO and protein produce water known as metabolic water when broken down for energy.

Normal levels of body water are maintained through kidney function. Loss of body water results in conservation by the kidneys while increased consumption leads to the kidneys ridding the body of excess water. Your body usually lets you know when you need water by thirst. In normal conditions, thirst is usually a good guide to body water needs and is effective in restoring body water to normal. Thirst is not a good indicator of body needs during exercise and especially when exercising in hot weather.

What Foods to Eat

To get adequate amounts of the nutrients listed above, you need to have a diet that include foods from the five major categories listed in the USDA chooseMyPlate.gov guide.

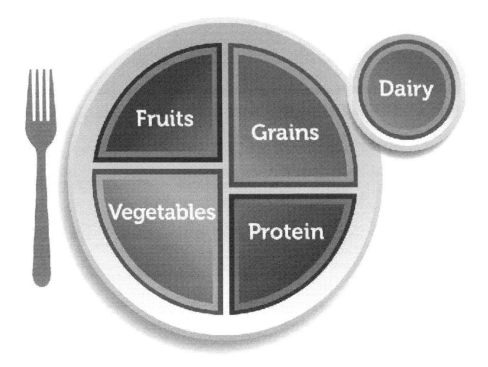

Grains
Breads, cereals, rice and pasta are the major sources of carbohydrates in this group; they also provide other nutrients such as thiamine, niacin and iron. Half of the grains you ingest should be whole grains such as oatmeal, whole wheat, cornmeal and brown rice. You should be eating more than 8 servings from this group daily.

Dairy Products
You should have 2 or more servings per day of milk, cheese, yogurt, cottage cheese or ice cream to provide calcium, riboflavin, protein and fat. To reduce the fat consumption, pick the low and non fat choices for all these dairy products. If you are not consuming any of these, make certain that you are getting some source of calcium in your diet. Calcium is essential in muscle contraction and endurance runners need about 1200 - 1500 mg per day.

Protein
You should have 2 or more servings per day of meat, fish, poultry, eggs, dry beans, legumes or nuts to provide protein, fat, niacin, iron and thiamine. Try to go lean with protein picking the lowest fat choices. Although many runners avoid red meat, it may be the best source of these nutrients making the once a week meal of super lean hamburger a good choice.

Fruits and Vegetables
You need 8 or more servings per day from these two groups to provide you with a good source of carbohydrates and vitamins particularly vitamins A & C. At least 2 servings should be fruits. Note that half your plate should consist of fruits and vegetables helping you get adequate intake of carbohydrates.

Junk Food (Fats, Oils and Sweets)
Cakes, cookies, pies, candy, soft drinks and alcoholic beverages consist mainly of simple carbohydrates and fat with minimal vitamin, mineral and other nutritional content. These foods should be eaten sparingly to supplement your caloric requirements after you have eaten the recommended servings from the other food groups.

Water
Don't forget that proper hydration is critical for performance. Significant decreases in performance occur after less than 45 minutes of exercise without water replacement. The average adult requires about 4 1/2 pints of water per day for normal metabolism. An additional pint per half hour may be lost during exercise. When exercising heavily in warm weather, you should be consuming fluids on a regular basis throughout your workout. Monitor your weight before and after the exercise and replace the fluid weight loss as soon after exercise as possible by consuming a about a pint per pound. You can determine your sweat rate by measuring weight before and after exercise, measuring the fluids consumed and the amount of urine loss. The weight loss divided by the exercise time is the sweat rate and can be used to learn your fluid needs.

Supplements

There is a huge vitamin, mineral, protein powder and other food supplement market. In general, if you eat a well balanced diet with adequate servings from all of the food groups listed above, supplements will only guarantee that you have expensive urine. There are of course, exceptions; for example, if you are lactose intolerant you need to take supplements to get adequate calcium. If you find you are craving salty foods after running in the heat, eat pretzels, saltines and some fruit to restore the potassium. Salt tablets are not recommended because they provide too concentrated a salt form which can impair athletic performance by drawing water out of the functioning muscle cells.

When to Eat

Pre Exercise

Pre exercise eating habits, especially before a race, vary tremendously from individual to individual. There are good reasons to eat before exercising. The main one is to prevent hypoglycemia (low blood sugar) that brings feelings of weakness, fatigue dizziness and nausea. There are some studies to show that eating lower glycemic index foods such as oatmeal, dairy products or fruit before exercise may be an advantage. The slower conversion to blood glucose allows slow release of energy and helps to stabilize blood sugar during exercise. Other reasons to eat are to settle your stomach, to keep from feeling hungry and to psychologically feel fueled and ready to go. Food eaten within one or two hours of exercise will not replenish glycogen stores. The timing and selection of foods are critical. Most athletes prefer the easy digestibility of high CHO, low fat foods such as breads, bagels, bananas and yogurt. Allow time for food to digest, at least 2- 4 hours before exercising. Avoid high sugar foods within 30 - 45 minutes of exercise as a quick insulin response will lead to hypoglycemia at the beginning of exercise. Sugar ingested immediately before exercise or during exercise will not elicit this insulin response. Drink 1 - 2 cups of water within 30 minutes before the start. You need to experiment during the training period especially before long runs to see what works for you.

During Exercise

There is a large body of scientific evidence that shows ingesting CHO during training or events that last longer than 2 hours will enhance performance and delay the onset of fatigue. As muscle glycogen stores become depleted, the body uses more blood sugar for energy. Liver glycogen stores support blood sugar level. Brain activities need blood sugar to sustain body functions. Endurance activity needs both mental and physical stamina. The blood sugar and liver glycogen levels can be maintained by the ingestion of CHO during exercise. High glycemic index foods such as glucose, glucose polymers ,sucrose or mix of these are the best choice. Individual responses to sports drinks, bars, gels, blocks or other concentrated forms of CHO vary. Read the labels and experiment with a variety to see what drinks or CHO choice works best for you. If you choose a concentrated form make certain you accompany it with adequate water to be able to empty it from the stomach. Most fruits, fruit juice and fructose containing sports drinks are med-low glycemic index foods making them a better pre or post exercise choice. Transport to the working muscles is improved using a glucose+fructose mix. Learn what aid will be offered by the marathon you are running and train with it. Start replacing CHO's early and replace on a regular basis. During training or marathons, ingest 100-200 calories worth of CHO every hour. Don't forget to drink adequate water to replace your sweat loss.

Post Exercise

An important aspect of training is post exercise glycogen (your carbohydrate energy source) replacement. Without muscle and liver glycogen resynthesis, the body will be chronically depleted and effective training becomes impossible. Training and racing may damage muscles which need repair plus stimulation to adapt to the training.

Recovery nutrition should include carbohydrate reloading, repairing and rebuilding new muscle tissue and rehydrating. The dietary factors that dictate the rate of muscle glycogen resynthesis are: the rate of carbohydrate ingestion, the timing of the carbohydrate ingestion after exercise and the carbohydrate type.

Glycogen resynthesis is at its highest immediately after exercise with a rate as high as 9% if 28 grams of carbohydrate is ingested every 15 minutes. It is important to start and optimize replacement within 30 minutes. Start with 0.5g CHO/lb of body weight, repeat within 2 hours. For runs 16 miles and longer repeat hourly for 3 hours. Add 10 -20 g protein as soon as possible to promote muscle tissue repair and adaptation.

After the first two hours, the maximum resynthesis rate is about 5%. This means that even with optimal replacement it will take a minimum of 1 day to replenish stores. After run of 16 miles and longer can take 2-3 days to replenish. To keep synthesis at maximum rates, carbohydrate ingestion needs to be at least 50 grams of carbohydrate every 2 hours. Eating much more than 50 grams will not increase the resynthesis rate.

High glycemic food such as glucose, sucrose (table sugar), maltodextrin, syrup, breads, raisins, and potatoes and moderate glycemic index foods such as rice, oatmeal, spaghetti, grapes, oranges and yams are equal at promoting resynthesis at optimal rates. Muscle glycogen resynthesis is about 3% per hour with low glycemic index foods such as most fruits, fructose (fruit sugar), most legumes (beans, etc) and dairy products.

A Suggested Strategy

Here is a suggested strategy to help you make certain that you are adequately fueled for your training.

First, determine your average daily calorie requirements by analyzing your BMR, activity level and training as discussed above.

Maintain a balanced training diet with 2 servings each from the milk and meat groups and at least 8 serving from each of the fruits and vegetables groups and the grains group. This should provide a minimum of 2000 -2500 calories per day.

To assure quick recovery from training, eat or drink the high glycemic carbohydrates in your diet immediately after workouts (up to 100 grams of carbohydrates in the first hour) and 50 g every 2 hours thereafter. A quick and nutritious way to replenish immediately is to drink 2 glasses (1 pint) of chocolate milk . The chocolate adds more carbohydrate calories to the milk which has adequate protein and contains leucine which signals the body to start protein synthesis and recovery. Chocolate soy milk works as well. The CHO/Protein ratio should 4:1 or 3:1 with carbohydrates the most needed.

If your caloric requirements are higher than the 2500 calories per day provided by the basic training diet, supplement with calories from high glycemic carbohydrate foods (ie bread) or drinks (ie Gatorade) making certain to get 50 grams (200 calories) every two hours after your workout. Note that some sports drinks are fructose based and are therefore not high glycemic.

Suppose your average workout day consists of a five mile run and your estimated calories consumption is 2500 calories. Your basic training diet would support this caloric requirement. In the first hour after your workout, you consume a large bagel (2 bread servings, 200 calories, high glycemic CHO) and a large glass of orange juice (2 fruit servings, 200 calories, moderate glycemic CHO). Every two hours for the next four hours, try to take in 2 servings of high to moderate glycemic carbohydrate foods, such as breads, potatoes and sports drinks along with plenty of water. This post exercise eating would account for half of your daily bread and fruit servings. The remainder of your nutritional needs should be consumed in your regular meals.

Suppose on a hard workout day you ran 10 miles. This would require about 500 more calories than your normal training diet. You could supplement that diet above by adding and additional 50 grams of high or moderate glycemic carbohydrate every 2 hours for the first four hours after your workout. This could be in the form of a quart of Gatorade or another bagel or better tasting 3-4 chocolate chip cookies, (animal crackers, graham crackers and fruit newtons have less fat, but might not be your choice).

Assess your sweat rate and replenish fluids on an as needed basis.

There are a number of books on sports nutrition available at the library or bookstore. For a more complete treatment at general nutrition, we recommend Jane Brody's Nutrition Book. If you are more interested in applications of nutrition to exercise and performance, choose Williams' Nutrition for Fitness and Sport, Clark's Sports Nutrition Guidebook , Coleman's Eating For Endurance or Girard Eberle's Eat, Drink Win.

Ergogenic Aids

Athletes are often searching for ways to gain a competitive "edge". Substances that are used to increase physical work capacity, or in this case, improve performance are termed ergogenic aids. To be effective, ergogenic aids must either help energy production, energy control or energy efficiency. Marathoning depends on the ability to sustain energy production at an optimal level for hours and to be efficient at the desired marathon pace. Ergogenic aids for the marathon must enhance energy utilization for the time span. Considerations for the use of an aid may be the timing and the possible detrimental effects plus the legal and ethical implications.

There are a number of ways to classify ergogenic aids and many aids cross several categories.

Nutritional Aids

The importance of good nutrition was covered in the Foods and Performance section. Carbohydrate loading is an ergogenic aid for events longer than 2 hours such as the marathon. A suggested method of loading in conjunction with tapering is discussed in the Race Preparation Section.

Taking fluid aid during the marathon is essential to good performance. The most important need during the marathon is for water replacement. Dehydration or loss of body water can disturb cardiovascular function, cell metabolism and temperature regulation. Water losses evidenced by a loss of 2% of body weight may lead to a significant decrease in endurance capacity. Water replenishment is imperative when running in the heat (See Food and Performance). Practice drinking during your training runs so that you are accustomed to running with liquid in your stomach and so that you can learn how to get it in. Assess your sweat rate so that you know exactly how much fluid you need.

While running the marathon, begin taking water at the first aid station. Drink at least one cup, preferably 2. If it is hot, pour another one over your head and shoulders. If you cannot drink while running, slow down and walk while you drink. The few seconds lost while drinking will easily be made up by feeling good throughout the race because you are well hydrated. Drink as much as you need to keep up with your sweat rate. Do not use thirst as a regulator of intake as the feeling of thirst does not keep up with the exercising body's need for water replacement. Water taken in after about the 22 mile point will probably not be used. However, the short rest and the psychological boost of a drink at that point may be important.

Glucose ingestion has been shown to be useful in events of over 1-1/2 to 2 hours such as the marathon. During the race, you usually have a choice of water and a glucose electrolyte solution. While the electrolytes are not always necessary, they contribute to feelings of thirst and act to increase intake. If you plan to drink the offered solution, purchase the same brand before the race and use it during your training runs. Never drink an unknown or untried solution during the race. Always take water with the solution that is offered because the body's greatest need is for water and the solution offered may be improperly mixed for optimal absorption. Too much sugar slows down the emptying of water from the stomach and too high concentration of electrolytes may cause intestinal cramps. If you are using gels, blocks or other concentrated sources of CHO, you need to make certain you take them with adequate water so they can empty from the stomach to the intestines to be absorbed. If you have problems drinking on the run or if the temperature is warmer than normal, you may benefit from hyperhydration. Drink a pint (2 cups) or more of water 15-30 minutes before the run. Practice this on training runs as well. Keep in mind that the water combined with pre-race nervousness may force you to stay close to the restrooms.

In prolonged events such as marathons, ultramarathons and longer triathlons, it may be necessary to replace electrolytes. Athletes in these events have been seen to develop hyponatremia, a condition with subnormal levels of sodium in the blood. The most common cause is overhydration. Athletes lose sodium through sweating and, if they consume excessive amounts of water, the body retains the water. Consequences include epileptic like seizures that can lead to death. To prevent this, solutions with small amounts (20-30meq/l) of salt are recommended. Check the label of the sports drink you are using to see the concentration contained. Individual differences in sweat rate dictate the amount of fluid needed.

Physiological Aids

Blood cell re-infusion or "doping" has been in the news after several Olympics. A controversy from the 1984 Olympics was the use of this technique by the American bicycling team. It led to the procedure being banned in 1985. Studies have shown that the procedure, properly done, can lead to a 10 - 15% increase in maximal oxygen uptake and an improvement in aerobic endurance.

The procedure consists of withdrawing a pint of an individual's blood 6-8 weeks before the event. That blood is stored and reinfused into the individual 1-2 days before the event. In the interim, the individual has restored normal red blood cell level and the addition boosts red blood cell count. The added blood cells and volume are theorized to contribute to a larger maximal heart output and increase the oxygen carrying capacity of the blood.

The glycoprotein hormone EPO (Erythropoietin) is also used to increase red blood cell production for performance enhancement. This drug was widely used by athletes during the 1990's. It is banned internationally from use by endurance athletes. A test was developed for EPO in 2000 and athletes are now routinely tested.

The added blood cells and volume are theorized to contribute to a larger maximal heart output and increase the oxygen carrying capacity of the blood. It is actually possible that doping may have opposite effects. The increase in the red blood cells could make the blood thicker and therefore, harder to pump through the body. There have been reported incidents of blood clots, strokes and possible deaths in athletes using blood doping techniques.

We mention blood doping here namely for your understanding of the process, but strongly discourage anyone from attempting it. You will increase your performance to a greater degree through intelligent training than you can through any techniques such as blood doping.

Carnitine is a physiological carrier that facilitates the transport of FFA's, (free fatty acids), to mitochondria. It would be useful if it increased the oxidation of FFA's and spared muscle glycogen. Studies have shown no actual effect on running performance either in oxygen consumption or in the use of FFA's as an energy source. There is no scientific basis for its use.

Alkaline salts are thought to benefit the athlete using the lactic acid system during exercise. The substance most often used is baking soda. It is theorized to help remove hydrogen ions to keep the proper muscle acid/base balance for enzyme function and energy production. Alkaline salts have not been shown to be of any benefit to endurance athletes including marathoners.

Phosphate salts are used in all of the energy production systems. Theoretically, phosphate salts could benefit performance in a wide range of events. Their effectiveness, as studied by numerous researchers, has not been demonstrated. Excess intake of phosphorus could contribute to calcium deficiency.

Pharmacological Aids

Stimulants

Studies about the effectiveness of anabolic steroids for improving performance are not all in agreement. The general results support the role of anabolic steroids to increase body weight, which can be mostly lean mass if the increase in training is supplemented with an increased protein intake. This is not usually a performance enhancer for marathoners. While steroids increased muscle mass, the studies evaluating their effectiveness in terms of increased strength and power have been variable. There are a number of studies showing no increase in maximal oxygen uptake or aerobic endurance performance. Neither have studies shown increases in facilitation of recovery in distance runners training daily at high levels. The newest anabolic agent, Human Growth Hormone (HGH) has not been thoroughly tested as to effectiveness in improving sports performance, but has shown dangerous side effects. Anabolic steroids are banned by most sports governing bodies, and, therefore, are not legal to use. They have extremely dangerous health risks that are exacerbated by long-term use. Do not use them!

Amphetamines or "pep pills" are also not indicated for usage in athletics. These pills are often taken by athletes to be "up" or psychologically ready. This is usually unnecessary and may result in drug dependency. Side effects such as headache, dizziness and masking the body's perception of pain, fatigue and heat stress are common and can actually hinder performance. Amphetamines are also on the list of banned substances.

Caffeine may or may not be a stimulant of value in endurance running. It acts as a central nervous system, heart rate and force stimulant, a smooth muscle relaxant, a stimulant for the release of adrenaline and will increase the amount of fatty acids in the blood. It may also increase the secretion of stomach acids and can act as a diuretic. Some recent research has shown that caffeine may be beneficial to performance in events lasting longer than 2 hours, such as the marathon. The caffeine elevates the free fatty acids in the blood and increases their utilization by the muscle for energy during the run. This action decreases the amount of muscle glycogen used, sparing muscle glycogen so that it can used better throughout the entire run. Other studies show that a high CHO diet and CHO loading may blunt any effects. Caffeine is a diuretic and can increase basal metabolic rate and heat production. These actions can contribute to inadequate temperature regulation in warm conditions   The body's response to caffeine is individual and caffeine drinks should be tried on training runs to discover your personal reaction. Certain individuals have strong adverse reactions to caffeine and should not use it. Caffeine is permitted by the International Olympic Committee, but only in limited amounts. To reach the limit, you would have to drink 5-6 cups of coffee in a short period of time.

Depressants

Alcohol does not seem to provide useful energy during exercise and may adversely affect physiologic processes important to energy metabolism during exercise. As a depressant, it may adversely affect perceptual-motor activities. The results of one or two drinks probably do not have any serious negative effects on performance, but recent studies have shown that during long distance running, alcohol may block the formation of glucose by the liver and decrease the release of glucose from the stomach. These actions may result in a decrease in blood glucose during the latter stages of the marathon. The most detrimental action is the disturbance of water balance in the muscle cells that could lead to a disturbance of cell enzyme activity with resultant increased fatigue. Light to moderate social drinking the evening prior to the event, but not on the same day, has not been shown to adversely effect physical performance. Overindulgence the night before may have the adverse effects listed above during the race if the alcohol has not been cleared from the system. Save the drinking of alcoholic beverages until after the race as your reward for a race well run. After the race, beer is a poor replacement source of CHO's with most of its calories derived from alcohol, which the body tends to metabolize as fat. Since beer has a diuretic effect, each beer consumed needs to be drunk in conjunction with 1-2 glasses of water to maintain fluid balance.

Tranquilizers have little effect either way on strength, power or anaerobic and aerobic endurance. They may affect performance that involves the need for quick judgements.

Beta-blockers may exert some adverse effects on aerobic endurance. They are valuable drugs for some heart and blood pressure problems. They act by decreasing heart response, blood flow to the muscle, and maximal oxygen uptake as well as blood levels of glucose and free fatty acid's.

Aspirin and Other Anti-Inflammatories

Painkillers and anti-inflammatories may or may not be ergogenic aids. Neither aspirin nor any other drug should be taken to mask specific pain before running. If something hurts enough to require a painkiller, you should consider not running and sparing your body more pain and added injury. The effects of anti-inflammatories to reduce swelling might be helpful in some cases. However, the latest research has shown that blocking inflammation slows the healing of injuries. Studies from Western Sates 100 runners show slower recovery times in those using anti-inflammatories during and after the run. If you have trouble sleeping after a marathon, a small dose of acetaminophen can be used before bedtime.

Running in Temperature Extremes

Performance may be influenced tremendously by temperature. As air temperature rises, the combination of environmental heat and increased body heat from exercise may result in bad effects ranging from decreased performance to death. Extreme cold, while usually not life threatening, can cause excessive body heat loss making good performance difficult.

The human body is able to maintain a fairly constant temperature under varying environmental conditions. To do this, it must be able to gain or lose heat. The core temperature is regulated to remain relatively constant, but the temperature of the shell, the skin and the tissues directly beneath it, varies directly with environmental conditions. The hypothalamus in the brain controls the body temperature and calls into play either heat loss or heat production mechanisms. Regulation comes in response to changes in the skin or blood temperature.

Normal metabolism in the body produces heat. Increased heat production can come from higher metabolic rates, disease, shivering or exercise. During exercise, the increased metabolic rate and energy production both generate heat. Most of the heat gain is due to the lack of efficiency of the body. It converts only 20-25% of energy produced into work; the rest is dissipated as heat.

Heat loss is governed by the following physical means.

> **Conduction:** transfer of heat from the body by direct physical contact.
> **Convection:** transfer of heat by movement of air or water over the body.
> **Radiation:** radiation of heat from the body into space.
> **Evaporation:** loss of heat by the body when converting sweat to vapor.

In a cold or cool environment, conduction and convection, along with some evaporation of sweat, can maintain the heat balance. As the temperature rises, evaporation of sweat becomes the main way of controlling the rise in core temperature. Evaporation can keep the body's exercising temperature in the normal range of 102-105 F under normal environmental circumstances.

Performance in Temperature Extremes

Several studies have shown that the optimum temperature for long distance running performance seems to be around 50-55 degrees Fahrenheit. Above and below this range performances degrade as much as 2% for every 5 degrees. Three additional environmental factors can interact to alter performance further. They are relative humidity, air movement, and radiation.

High humidity, because it inhibits evaporation, has the same effect as increasing the ambient temperature. This effect is worse for higher temperatures where it can increase the effective ambient temperature by as much as 10 degrees.

Air movement over the body enhances the ability to lose heat by convection and evaporation. Movement is generated both by the runner's speed and by any prevailing wind. These can combine to lower the effective temperature by as much as 8 or 9 degrees while increasing evaporation and fluid loss. Running downwind cancels out this cooling effect.

Direct sunlight adds heat to the body by radiation. The effective temperature increase can be as much as 8 or 9 degrees.

It is easy to see that by combining 80+ degree temperatures with direct sun exposure and high humidity serious performance degradation will occur in long distance races.

Heat Illnesses

Special caution should be advised when the temperature is above 80 F or when the relative humidity exceeds 50-60%.

Running unwisely under environmental heat stress may lead to a variety of heat illnesses which can be life threatening. These illnesses are caused by three factors: increased core temperature, loss of body fluids, and loss of electrolytes. While running in the heat, monitor your condition for signs of weakness, dizziness, nausea, disorientation, cessation of sweating and piloerection, the standing up of body hairs. If these signs occur, stop running and start the appropriate treatment. They could be symptoms of any of the major heat illnesses described below.

>**Heat Cramps:** Salts can be lost in the sweat while running in the heat. If they are not replenished properly, muscle pain and cramps can occur. The body temperature does not become elevated. Prevention can come from heat acclimatization, ingestion of large amounts of water and by increasing the daily salt intake several days before the heat stress. Treatment is rest in a cool environment and replacement of lost salts.
>
>**Heat Exhaustion:** Poor circulatory response to heat and reduction of blood volume due to increased sweating can lead to symptoms of general weakness, dizziness and nausea. The skin is usually cool and pale, but the person is probably still sweating. Body temperature is not elevated to dangerous levels (under 106F). Exercise must be stopped. Treat by rest in a cool environment, ingestion of cool liquids and cooling the body externally with water or ice.
>
>**Heat Stroke:** When the body's temperature regulating system fails, excessively high body temperature and heat stroke can result. This is a serious condition that, if untreated, may well lead to death. It requires immediate medical attention. The symptoms are dry, warm and red skin, a reduction or loss of sweat and a body core temperature over 106F. Treatment is to immediately stop exercise, seek medical attention and start cooling the body with ice packs and cold water. The person may or may not be conscious. Cool liquids may be consumed if the person is conscious.

There are ways to reduce hazards when running in the heat and/or humidity. Most are common sense:

1. Check the conditions before exercising and adjust your plan if needed. Slow the pace or decrease the duration of activity if training when hot or humid. If racing when hot and humid, realize that performance will be less than expected. If the event is not a key one, relax and save the bigger effort for a cooler day.
2. Run in the early morning or late evening to avoid the heat of the day. In many climates, late afternoon is the hottest time of the day and running then should be avoided.
3. Find a shady road or trail to run on.
4. Dress accordingly; wear as few clothes as you decently can. Try loose fitting white shorts and a white mesh top to reflect the heat and to permit evaporation. Protect your head from intense sun with a lightweight hat that can breathe. A hat or a cotton kerchief can protect the back of the neck. Ice can be wrapped in the kerchief and carried under the hat.
5. Drink fluids while running. Carry a water bottle or pick a route with water fountains. Drink 4-8 oz. of water for every 15-20 minutes of running or enough to replenish based on your sweat rate. Also pour water over your head and chest.
6. Weigh yourself after workouts and replenish lost water. Body weight should be back to normal before the next workout.
7. Try hyperhydration by drinking 2-4 cups of water 30 minutes before running.
8. Be aware of lost electrolytes if you've sweated excessively. Put an appropriate amount salt on foods and eat bananas and citrus fruit.
9. Avoid excess protein intake. Protein metabolism produces extra heat.
10. Know the signs and symptoms of heat illness and their treatments. If you have any of the symptoms, stop running, get to a cool place and consume cold fluids.
11. If you are going to compete in an event in hot conditions, acclimatize first.

Heat Acclimatization

With proper heat acclimatization, the body can perform as if it were in temperatures 10 to 15 degrees Fahrenheit cooler. Acclimatization is the process of adapting your body to be able to run more efficiently under hot environmental conditions. When it is hot the blood goes to the skin for cooling the body as well as to the working muscles. This increases the workload of the heart and the exercising heart rate. Intensity of exercise will need to be reduced when running in the heat and when acclimatizing for proper adaptation.

The body makes several adjustments during the heat acclimatization process. The circulatory adaptations to acclimatization provide better transport of heat from the core to the skin. There is better distribution of the blood to regulate temperature. This frees a greater portion of the heart output for the working muscles. Sweating mechanisms undergo complementary changes. Sweating starts at a lower body temperature and the capacity for sweating nearly doubles. The sweat becomes more dilute, contains less salt, and is more evenly distributed over the skin. Major changes occur during the first week of heat exposure and are mostly complete after 14 days. Beyond 14 days long term (for 6 months or longer) improvements in cooling efficiency are evident in reduction of sweating needed to regulate temperature. These are likely a benefit for longer events such as a marathon where hydration is an important factor.

Heat acclimatization can also be lost in 14 days. This is why it is important to wear extra clothing during unusually cool summer weather. You should try to maintain acclimatization for typical hot weather conditions that could occur on short notice at your next race.

The ways to acclimatize are:

- Begin early in the season when the temperature is moderate and wear one more layer of clothing than usual on 3 runs per week. If you would normally wear a T-shirt wear a long sleeved one or a jacket. This technique provides a hot, humid micro-atmosphere and prevents evaporation. This early constant acclimatization works well in climates such as in Oregon where the weather is often unpredictable and occasional hot days are experienced relatively early in the year.
- To develop and maintain acclimatization in weather that is unseasonably cool or in preparing for a race in a warmer climate assume that each layer of dry clothing or degree of coverage, (i.e. going from short to long sleeved shirt or from shorts to tights), is equivalent to 15 or 20 degrees in temperature. Adding a waterproof jacket such as Tyvec provides a hot, humid micro-atmosphere and prevents evaporation that would normally cool you once your clothes became wet.
- If the weather suddenly turns hot, reduce the training load; run slower and less distance. Slowly build back up to usual mileage and intensity. Work on heat acclimatization every other day and make certain to replace lost fluids. Run in the cooler part of the day on the non acclimatization days. Do not overdo and get heat symptoms.
- If you plan to race under hot conditions, remember that acclimatization takes about 10 days. Plan to be acclimatized a week in advance. During the week before the event, avoid extra heat stress that may dehydrate and fatigue you for the race.
- Make sure you adequately hydrate yourself when you are heat acclimatizing. This will prevent injury and train your body to use fluids.

Fluid and Electrolyte Replacement

Optimal performance depends on proper hydration. Dehydration or excessive loss of body water reduces the amount of time you can exercise as well as necessitating slowing down. Changes that take place at the cellular level adversely effect muscle contraction. Water losses of 2% or more of body weight impair circulatory function and create heat imbalance. You should drink enough to replace the fluid lost by sweating ; a 4-8 ounces of fluid every 15-20 minutes during exercise is a reasonable guideline. You can also hyperhydrate by drinking 2-4 cups of cold fluid 15-30 minutes before exercise.

Sweat is comprised mainly of water and sodium and chloride ions. These ions are known as electrolytes. Other electrolytes are also present in small amounts. Studies of electrolyte balance during and after exercise have shown increases in the electrolytes in the blood, but these changes are probably due to water loss and muscle use.

There is evidence that glucose electrolyte solutions (sports drinks) help replenish body water better than plain water. While the electrolytes are probably not necessary for replacement in runs shorter than a marathon, they improve fluid absorption by the body and encourage further drinking by stimulating the bodies thirst mechanism. In runs longer than 90 minutes, the carbohydrate in sports drinks helps spare liver glycogen depletion. For optimum absorption drinks should contain 5 to 10% carbohydrate (glucose or sucrose) and should be cool (40-50 degrees F). For longer runs it is also important to maintain electrolyte balance (see Hyponatremia below). So replacement drinks containing sodium or ingestion of salt may be desirable.

If running in the heat for several consecutive days, try to replace fluids and eat a balanced diet. Add salt to foods and select foods high in potassium such as bananas and citrus fruits. Salt tablets are unnecessary and may be harmful when not taken with adequate water.

Hyponatremia

When excess amounts of water are consumed and/or large amounts of sodium are lost in the sweat or urine a condition know as hyponatremia (low sodium) can occur. This is a situation where sodium levels in the blood become too dilute to properly support normal cell metabolism. Symptoms ranging from headache and nausea to seizures and death can occur.

Too avoid hyponatremia, drink replacement fluids containing sodium vs. straight water, moderate your drinking and train adequately for your event and conditions.

Running in the Cold

Cold is usually not as hazardous for the runner as is heat. With exercise metabolism, the body is able to maintain a constant core temperature in air temperatures as low as - 22F. This is regulated by internal mechanisms and not necessarily by the heat produced from exercise. Shivering can be seen during exercise when the core temperature is low. Under this stress, oxygen consumption is higher than when doing the same amount of exercise in warm weather.

Common sense tells you to be comfortable while running; this is also true in cold weather. Both body fat and clothing act as heat conserving mechanisms. High body fat is not conducive to good performance and is not common in runners, so most must learn to dress warmly. It is often difficult to determine how many clothes to wear in winter conditions. The heat generated by your body can be seven or eight times as great when running as it is at rest leading some runners to overdress at the start of their run. On the other hand, if you are dressed to be "just right" when you are running hard and you must slow down or walk due to fatigue or injury, you risk the threat of hypothermia. When you couple this variation in the body's heat generating capability with the rapid changes possible in winter weather and the loss of insulating properties of clothing when it is wet, the following guidelines emerge.

- You are better off to overdress than underdress. Very few people die from overheating in the winter, many from hypothermia.
- The more adaptable clothing is the better. Layers of clothing trap and warm the air between them acting as insulation. You should use layers that you can remove as you get warmer and add as you get colder and clothing which can be zipped, buttoned, rolled up or down to provide more or less cooling.
- You should attempt to stay as dry as possible. If clothing becomes wet either through sweating or external sources (rain, snow), it can conduct heat away from the body. Regulate your clothing so it doesn't become sweat soaked, use materials such as thermax or poly-pro which wick moisture away from your skin as you sweat, and wear a rainproof shell which sheds moisture and does not soak it up when it is precipitating.

When deciding what to wear for your run, first check the temperature as well as the conditions outside. Running with bare legs in cold weather is not advised. The red color of the skin shows that a great deal of the blood is detoured to the skin trying to keep the body warm and is not going to the exercising muscles where it is needed most. Cold muscles feel tight and are more susceptible to injury, especially pulls and strains. We suggest lycra tights or other leg covering when the temperature is below 40. Many options in materials for tights are available, from water resistant to extra warm fuzzy polypro that can be worn as the conditions change. Fabrics that are waterproof, but can still breathe are best for external layers. Gortex works quite well, if you don't sweat a great deal. Polypropylene is excellent next to the skin as it wicks away the water and allows a warm air layer to remain. A major part of heat loss is through the head, so wear a hat or ski headband to help keep warm. Gloves are important as well and range from cotton to polypro to gortex. If it's wet, polypro keeps hands much warmer and the gortex mittens on top on a rainy day are a sheer indulgence. You can remove gloves, hat or layers of clothing as you become warmer. Check your local running store for the latest in winter running fabrics.

Safety Concerns

After daylight savings time is over, many of us run mostly in the dark. The dark presents a number of safety problems. It is also sometimes raining when it's dark, making runner visibility to cars very difficult. It is important to wear apparel that can be seen by motorists and cyclists. The best is a reflective vest. Jackets, T-shirts, tights and shoes can be purchased with reflective strips. Highly visible lightweight flashing lights are also available. The most visible spots for reflective material seem to be on the moving parts such as shoes, legs and arms. Not all shoes come with reflective strips or the newest "flashing lights", but you can buy stick on reflective materials.

The best places to run are areas where it's lighted. Seek out well lighted streets used by runners in your area. Many tracks have runner lights that can be turned on.

It makes sense to run apart from cars, such as on a bike path or the sidewalk. **Always** run facing traffic so as not get hit from behind. The most dangerous crossing is in front of a car turning with the driver only checking out what's coming from the opposite direction. Never step in front of this car without recognition from the driver. It is wiser to assume they don't see you and run behind the car.

With the advent of mobile phones and entertainment devices came a new hazard, distraction. You must be more aware of distracted drivers who may be more interested in a phone conversation than watching for you. Listening to your tunes or phone may be fun, but it also keeps you from hearing impending dangers. **Never** run on the road with cars, alone or in the dark with headphones. They are great for treadmills and the gym.

Women face more safety problems and must always be careful when running alone. The early morning hours seem to be a time when perverts are out. The best ideas are to run only in areas that you know are safe, and run with a companion or companions. Never run with headphones in the dark, in areas of questionable safety or with your back to traffic. Try to hook up with other runners or get a canine companion. Dogs can be fun to run with and great protection. They need to be trained for endurance, should run on a leash and never disagree with you. It would be a good idea to sign up for a personal safety program offered in your area.

Appendices

Example Training Log

A simple training log is useful for laying out your program and monitoring your progress. The one given below is an example. You can devise a similar form of your own. If you lay out one on a single sheet of paper you can copy it and use a loose-leaf notebook to store enough weeks for your entire training plan. You could also devise a simple spread sheet to hold your information. Fill out your workout schedules several weeks into the future, planning around things such as races, appointments etc.

Each day log your resting pulse (HR), your weight, general health (1-5 scale), and when you went to bed. After your workout log your recovery pulse (HR), time and any other comments. You can refer to your log to monitor your progress, to determine where things went right or wrong or to look for signs of overtraining.

Schedule For:				Month:

SUN	Plan	Actual	Pulse: Weight: Health: Bed Hr:	Comments

MON	Plan	Actual	Pulse: Weight: Health: Bed Hr:	Comments

TUE	Plan	Actual	Pulse: Weight: Health: Bed Hr:	Comments

WED	Plan	Actual	Pulse: Weight: Health: Bed Hr:	Comments

THU	Plan	Actual	Pulse: Weight: Health: Bed Hr:	Comments

FRI	Plan	Actual	Pulse: Weight: Health: Bed Hr:	Comments

SAT	Plan	Actual	Pulse: Weight: Health: Bed Hr:	Comments

Pace Tables

The following pages contain tables of running paces for various race and training distances. Each column represents a constant level of ability over various distances for a runner. Thus all a runner's race and training times should theoretically appear in the same vertical column. Each column in the tables going to the right represents approximately a 2% decrease in ability. The numbers on the top line of the table are estimates of the maximal oxygen consumption VO2 Max in ml/kg-min for runners who match the race times in those columns. The first column in the chart is consistent with current men's world class performances.

For each distance in the table, three times are listed. The top time is the total elapsed time for the distance. The middle time is the pace per mile. The bottom time is the pace per 400 meters, (1 lap on a standard track).

Using the table:

- The first thing to do is to find your current race times in the table and establish the column which most closely represents the best of your times. This column has your estimated VO2max at the top.

Using the table for racing:

- Within your column are estimated times and race paces for any race distances listed. Thus you can use the table to establish target paces for these distances.

Using the table for training:

- At the bottom of your column highlighted in light gray are easy, (80% effort), running paces for various endurance training runs. These paces are appropriate for base building runs and on easy days.

- The upper two (race) sections of your column highlighted in medium and light gray are running paces which are appropriate for interval or pace training at different race intensities.

VO2:		84.8	82.9	81.1	79.3	77.5	75.8	74.2
2mi	race	8:00	8:10	8:21	8:33	8:44	8:56	9:08
		4:00	4:05	4:10	4:16	4:22	4:28	4:34
		1:00	1:01	1:02	1:04	1:05	1:07	1:08
5km	race	12:49	13:06	13:24	13:42	14:00	14:19	14:38
		4:07	4:13	4:18	4:24	4:30	4:36	4:42
		1:01	1:03	1:04	1:06	1:07	1:09	1:10
5mi	race	21:19	21:48	22:17	22:47	23:18	23:50	24:22
		4:15	4:21	4:27	4:33	4:39	4:46	4:52
		1:03	1:05	1:06	1:08	1:09	1:11	1:13
10km	race	26:54	27:30	28:08	28:45	29:24	30:04	30:45
		4:19	4:25	4:31	4:37	4:44	4:50	4:56
		1:04	1:06	1:07	1:09	1:11	1:12	1:14
15km	race	41:31	42:27	43:24	44:23	45:23	46:24	47:27
		4:27	4:33	4:39	4:45	4:52	4:58	5:05
		1:06	1:08	1:09	1:11	1:13	1:14	1:16
10mi	race	44:46	45:46	46:48	47:51	48:56	50:02	51:09
		4:28	4:34	4:40	4:47	4:53	5:00	5:06
		1:07	1:08	1:10	1:11	1:13	1:15	1:16
20km	race	56:29	57:45	59:03	1:00:23	1:01:45	1:03:08	1:04:33
		4:32	4:38	4:45	4:51	4:58	5:04	5:11
		1:08	1:09	1:11	1:12	1:14	1:16	1:17
13.1mi	race	59:49	1:01:09	1:02:32	1:03:56	1:05:23	1:06:51	1:08:21
		4:33	4:39	4:46	4:52	4:59	5:05	5:12
		1:08	1:09	1:11	1:13	1:14	1:16	1:18
25km	race	1:11:43	1:13:20	1:14:59	1:16:40	1:18:24	1:20:10	1:21:58
		4:37	4:43	4:49	4:56	5:02	5:09	5:16
		1:09	1:10	1:12	1:14	1:15	1:17	1:19
30km	race	1:27:10	1:29:08	1:31:08	1:33:11	1:35:17	1:37:26	1:39:37
		4:40	4:46	4:53	4:59	5:06	5:13	5:20
		1:10	1:11	1:13	1:14	1:16	1:18	1:20
Marthn	race	2:05:34	2:08:24	2:11:17	2:14:15	2:17:16	2:20:21	2:23:31
		4:47	4:53	5:00	5:07	5:14	5:21	5:28
		1:11	1:13	1:15	1:16	1:18	1:20	1:22
< 6mi	train	32:23	33:07	33:52	34:38	35:24	36:12	37:01
		5:23	5:31	5:38	5:46	5:54	6:02	6:10
		1:20	1:22	1:24	1:26	1:28	1:30	1:32
10mi	train	55:57	57:13	58:30	59:49	1:01:10	1:02:32	1:03:57
		5:35	5:43	5:51	5:58	6:07	6:15	6:23
		1:23	1:25	1:27	1:29	1:31	1:33	1:35
15mi	train	1:26:21	1:28:18	1:30:17	1:32:19	1:34:23	1:36:31	1:38:41
		5:45	5:53	6:01	6:09	6:17	6:26	6:34
		1:26	1:28	1:30	1:32	1:34	1:36	1:38
20mi	train	1:57:29	2:00:07	2:02:50	2:05:36	2:08:25	2:11:18	2:14:16
		5:52	6:00	6:08	6:16	6:25	6:33	6:42
		1:28	1:30	1:32	1:34	1:36	1:38	1:40

VO2:	72.5	70.9	69.4	67.9	66.4	64.9	63.5
2mi race	9:20	9:33	9:46	9:59	10:13	10:26	10:41
	4:40	4:46	4:53	4:59	5:06	5:13	5:20
	1:10	1:11	1:13	1:14	1:16	1:18	1:20
5km race	14:58	15:18	15:39	16:00	16:22	16:44	17:06
	4:49	4:55	5:02	5:09	5:16	5:23	5:30
	1:12	1:13	1:15	1:17	1:19	1:20	1:22
5mi race	24:55	25:28	26:03	26:38	27:14	27:51	28:28
	4:59	5:05	5:12	5:19	5:26	5:34	5:41
	1:14	1:16	1:18	1:19	1:21	1:23	1:25
10km race	31:26	32:09	32:52	33:36	34:22	35:08	35:56
	5:03	5:10	5:17	5:24	5:31	5:39	5:46
	1:15	1:17	1:19	1:21	1:22	1:24	1:26
15km race	48:31	49:36	50:43	51:52	53:02	54:14	55:27
	5:12	5:19	5:26	5:33	5:41	5:49	5:56
	1:18	1:19	1:21	1:23	1:25	1:27	1:29
10mi race	52:18	53:29	54:41	55:55	57:11	58:28	59:47
	5:13	5:20	5:28	5:35	5:43	5:50	5:58
	1:18	1:20	1:22	1:23	1:25	1:27	1:29
20km race	1:06:00	1:07:29	1:09:01	1:10:34	1:12:09	1:13:46	1:15:26
	5:18	5:25	5:33	5:40	5:48	5:56	6:04
	1:19	1:21	1:23	1:25	1:27	1:29	1:31
13.1mi race	1:09:53	1:11:28	1:13:04	1:14:43	1:16:24	1:18:07	1:19:52
	5:19	5:27	5:34	5:41	5:49	5:57	6:05
	1:19	1:21	1:23	1:25	1:27	1:29	1:31
25km race	1:23:49	1:25:42	1:27:37	1:29:36	1:31:37	1:33:40	1:35:47
	5:23	5:31	5:38	5:46	5:53	6:01	6:09
	1:20	1:22	1:24	1:26	1:28	1:30	1:32
30km race	1:41:52	1:44:09	1:46:30	1:48:54	1:51:21	1:53:51	1:56:25
	5:27	5:35	5:42	5:50	5:58	6:06	6:14
	1:21	1:23	1:25	1:27	1:29	1:31	1:33
Marthn race	2:26:44	2:30:02	2:33:25	2:36:52	2:40:24	2:44:00	2:47:42
	5:35	5:43	5:51	5:58	6:07	6:15	6:23
	1:23	1:25	1:27	1:29	1:31	1:33	1:35
< 6mi train	37:51	38:42	39:34	40:28	41:22	42:18	43:15
	6:18	6:27	6:35	6:44	6:53	7:03	7:12
	1:34	1:36	1:38	1:41	1:43	1:45	1:48
10mi train	1:05:23	1:06:51	1:08:22	1:09:54	1:11:28	1:13:05	1:14:44
	6:32	6:41	6:50	6:59	7:08	7:18	7:28
	1:38	1:40	1:42	1:44	1:47	1:49	1:52
15mi train	1:40:54	1:43:11	1:45:30	1:47:52	1:50:18	1:52:47	1:55:19
	6:43	6:52	7:02	7:11	7:21	7:31	7:41
	1:40	1:43	1:45	1:47	1:50	1:52	1:55
20mi train	2:17:17	2:20:22	2:23:32	2:26:46	2:30:04	2:33:26	2:36:54
	6:51	7:01	7:10	7:20	7:30	7:40	7:50
	1:42	1:45	1:47	1:50	1:52	1:55	1:57

VO2:		62.1	60.7	59.4	58.1	56.8	55.5	54.3
2mi	race	10:55	11:10	11:25	11:40	11:56	12:12	12:29
		5:27	5:35	5:42	5:50	5:58	6:06	6:14
		1:21	1:23	1:25	1:27	1:29	1:31	1:33
5km	race	17:30	17:53	18:17	18:42	19:07	19:33	20:00
		5:37	5:45	5:53	6:01	6:09	6:17	6:26
		1:24	1:26	1:28	1:30	1:32	1:34	1:36
5mi	race	29:07	29:46	30:26	31:07	31:49	32:32	33:16
		5:49	5:57	6:05	6:13	6:21	6:30	6:39
		1:27	1:29	1:31	1:33	1:35	1:37	1:39
10km	race	36:44	37:34	38:24	39:16	40:09	41:04	41:59
		5:54	6:02	6:10	6:19	6:27	6:36	6:45
		1:28	1:30	1:32	1:34	1:36	1:39	1:41
15km	race	56:42	57:58	59:16	1:00:36	1:01:58	1:03:22	1:04:48
		6:04	6:13	6:21	6:30	6:38	6:47	6:57
		1:31	1:33	1:35	1:37	1:39	1:41	1:44
10mi	race	1:01:07	1:02:30	1:03:54	1:05:21	1:06:49	1:08:19	1:09:51
		6:06	6:15	6:23	6:32	6:40	6:49	6:59
		1:31	1:33	1:35	1:38	1:40	1:42	1:44
20km	race	1:17:08	1:18:52	1:20:39	1:22:27	1:24:19	1:26:13	1:28:09
		6:12	6:20	6:29	6:38	6:47	6:56	7:05
		1:33	1:35	1:37	1:39	1:41	1:44	1:46
13.1mi	race	1:21:40	1:23:30	1:25:23	1:27:19	1:29:16	1:31:17	1:33:20
		6:13	6:22	6:30	6:39	6:48	6:57	7:07
		1:33	1:35	1:37	1:39	1:42	1:44	1:46
25km	race	1:37:56	1:40:08	1:42:24	1:44:42	1:47:03	1:49:28	1:51:55
		6:18	6:26	6:35	6:44	6:53	7:02	7:12
		1:34	1:36	1:38	1:41	1:43	1:45	1:48
30km	race	1:59:02	2:01:43	2:04:27	2:07:15	2:10:07	2:13:03	2:16:02
		6:23	6:31	6:40	6:49	6:58	7:08	7:17
		1:35	1:37	1:40	1:42	1:44	1:47	1:49
Marthn	race	2:51:28	2:55:20	2:59:16	3:03:18	3:07:26	3:11:39	3:15:58
		6:32	6:41	6:50	6:59	7:08	7:18	7:28
		1:38	1:40	1:42	1:44	1:47	1:49	1:52
< 6mi	train	44:14	45:14	46:15	47:17	48:21	49:26	50:33
		7:22	7:32	7:42	7:52	8:03	8:14	8:25
		1:50	1:53	1:55	1:58	2:00	2:03	2:06
10mi	train	1:16:24	1:18:08	1:19:53	1:21:41	1:23:31	1:25:24	1:27:19
		7:38	7:48	7:59	8:10	8:21	8:32	8:43
		1:54	1:57	1:59	2:02	2:05	2:08	2:10
15mi	train	1:57:55	2:00:34	2:03:17	2:06:03	2:08:54	2:11:48	2:14:45
		7:51	8:02	8:13	8:24	8:35	8:47	8:59
		1:57	2:00	2:03	2:06	2:08	2:11	2:14
20mi	train	2:40:25	2:44:02	2:47:43	2:51:30	2:55:21	2:59:18	3:03:20
		8:01	8:12	8:23	8:34	8:46	8:57	9:10
		2:00	2:03	2:05	2:08	2:11	2:14	2:17

VO2:		53.1	52.0	50.8	49.7	48.6	47.5	46.5
2mi	race	12:45	13:03	13:20	13:38	13:57	14:16	14:35
		6:22	6:31	6:40	6:49	6:58	7:08	7:17
		1:35	1:37	1:40	1:42	1:44	1:47	1:49
5km	race	20:27	20:54	21:22	21:51	22:21	22:51	23:22
		6:34	6:43	6:52	7:02	7:11	7:21	7:31
		1:38	1:40	1:43	1:45	1:47	1:50	1:52
5mi	race	34:01	34:47	35:34	36:22	37:11	38:01	38:53
		6:48	6:57	7:06	7:16	7:26	7:36	7:46
		1:42	1:44	1:46	1:49	1:51	1:54	1:56
10km	race	42:56	43:54	44:53	45:54	46:55	47:59	49:04
		6:54	7:03	7:13	7:23	7:33	7:43	7:53
		1:43	1:45	1:48	1:50	1:53	1:55	1:58
15km	race	1:06:15	1:07:44	1:09:16	1:10:49	1:12:25	1:14:03	1:15:43
		7:06	7:16	7:25	7:35	7:46	7:56	8:07
		1:46	1:49	1:51	1:53	1:56	1:59	2:01
10mi	race	1:11:26	1:13:02	1:14:41	1:16:22	1:18:05	1:19:50	1:21:38
		7:08	7:18	7:28	7:38	7:48	7:59	8:09
		1:47	1:49	1:52	1:54	1:57	1:59	2:02
20km	race	1:30:08	1:32:10	1:34:14	1:36:21	1:38:31	1:40:44	1:43:00
		7:15	7:24	7:34	7:45	7:55	8:06	8:17
		1:48	1:51	1:53	1:56	1:58	2:01	2:04
13.1mi	race	1:35:26	1:37:35	1:39:47	1:42:02	1:44:19	1:46:40	1:49:04
		7:16	7:26	7:36	7:46	7:57	8:08	8:19
		1:49	1:51	1:54	1:56	1:59	2:02	2:04
25km	race	1:54:27	1:57:01	1:59:39	2:02:21	2:05:06	2:07:55	2:10:47
		7:22	7:31	7:42	7:52	8:03	8:14	8:25
		1:50	1:52	1:55	1:58	2:00	2:03	2:06
30km	race	2:19:06	2:22:14	2:25:26	2:28:42	2:32:03	2:35:28	2:38:58
		7:27	7:37	7:48	7:58	8:09	8:20	8:31
		1:51	1:54	1:57	1:59	2:02	2:05	2:07
Marthn	race	3:20:22	3:24:53	3:29:29	3:34:12	3:39:01	3:43:57	3:48:59
		7:38	7:48	7:59	8:10	8:21	8:32	8:44
		1:54	1:57	1:59	2:02	2:05	2:08	2:11
< 6mi	train	51:41	52:51	54:02	55:15	56:30	57:46	59:04
		8:36	8:48	9:00	9:12	9:25	9:37	9:50
		2:09	2:12	2:15	2:18	2:21	2:24	2:27
10mi	train	1:29:17	1:31:18	1:33:21	1:35:27	1:37:36	1:39:48	1:42:02
		8:55	9:07	9:20	9:32	9:45	9:58	10:12
		2:13	2:16	2:20	2:23	2:26	2:29	2:33
15mi	train	2:17:47	2:20:53	2:24:04	2:27:18	2:30:37	2:34:00	2:37:28
		9:11	9:23	9:36	9:49	10:02	10:16	10:29
		2:17	2:20	2:24	2:27	2:30	2:34	2:37
20mi	train	3:07:28	3:11:41	3:16:00	3:20:24	3:24:55	3:29:31	3:34:14
		9:22	9:35	9:48	10:01	10:14	10:28	10:42
		2:20	2:23	2:27	2:30	2:33	2:37	2:40

VO2:		45.5	44.5	43.5	42.5	41.6	40.7	39.8
2mi	race	14:54	15:15	15:35	15:56	16:18	16:40	17:02
		7:27	7:37	7:47	7:58	8:09	8:20	8:31
		1:51	1:54	1:56	1:59	2:02	2:05	2:07
5km	race	23:53	24:26	24:59	25:32	26:07	26:42	27:18
		7:41	7:51	8:02	8:13	8:24	8:35	8:47
		1:55	1:57	2:00	2:03	2:06	2:08	2:11
5mi	race	39:45	40:39	41:34	42:30	43:27	44:26	45:26
		7:57	8:07	8:18	8:30	8:41	8:53	9:05
		1:59	2:01	2:04	2:07	2:10	2:13	2:16
10km	race	50:10	51:18	52:27	53:38	54:50	56:04	57:20
		8:04	8:15	8:26	8:37	8:49	9:01	9:13
		2:01	2:03	2:06	2:09	2:12	2:15	2:18
15km	race	1:17:25	1:19:10	1:20:56	1:22:46	1:24:37	1:26:32	1:28:29
		8:18	8:29	8:41	8:52	9:04	9:17	9:29
		2:04	2:07	2:10	2:13	2:16	2:19	2:22
10mi	race	1:23:28	1:25:21	1:27:16	1:29:14	1:31:14	1:33:17	1:35:23
		8:20	8:32	8:43	8:55	9:07	9:19	9:32
		2:05	2:08	2:10	2:13	2:16	2:19	2:23
20km	race	1:45:20	1:47:42	1:50:07	1:52:36	1:55:08	1:57:43	2:00:22
		8:28	8:39	8:51	9:03	9:15	9:28	9:41
		2:07	2:09	2:12	2:15	2:18	2:22	2:25
13.1mi	race	1:51:31	1:54:02	1:56:36	1:59:13	2:01:54	2:04:39	2:07:27
		8:30	8:41	8:53	9:05	9:17	9:30	9:43
		2:07	2:10	2:13	2:16	2:19	2:22	2:25
25km	race	2:13:44	2:16:44	2:19:49	2:22:58	2:26:11	2:29:28	2:32:50
		8:36	8:48	9:00	9:12	9:24	9:37	9:50
		2:09	2:12	2:15	2:18	2:21	2:24	2:27
30km	race	2:42:33	2:46:12	2:49:56	2:53:46	2:57:40	3:01:40	3:05:45
		8:43	8:54	9:06	9:19	9:31	9:44	9:57
		2:10	2:13	2:16	2:19	2:22	2:26	2:29
Marthn	race	3:54:09	3:59:25	4:04:48	4:10:18	4:15:56	4:21:42	4:27:35
		8:55	9:07	9:20	9:32	9:45	9:58	10:12
		2:13	2:16	2:20	2:23	2:26	2:29	2:33
< 6mi	train	1:00:24	1:01:46	1:03:09	1:04:34	1:06:01	1:07:30	1:09:02
		10:04	10:17	10:31	10:45	11:00	11:15	11:30
		2:31	2:34	2:37	2:41	2:45	2:48	2:52
10mi	train	1:44:20	1:46:41	1:49:05	1:51:32	1:54:03	1:56:37	1:59:14
		10:26	10:40	10:54	11:09	11:24	11:39	11:55
		2:36	2:40	2:43	2:47	2:51	2:54	2:58
15mi	train	2:41:01	2:44:38	2:48:21	2:52:08	2:56:00	2:59:58	3:04:01
		10:44	10:58	11:13	11:28	11:44	11:59	12:16
		2:41	2:44	2:48	2:52	2:56	2:59	3:04
20mi	train	3:39:03	3:43:59	3:49:02	3:54:11	3:59:27	4:04:50	4:10:21
		10:57	11:11	11:27	11:42	11:58	12:14	12:31
		2:44	2:47	2:51	2:55	2:59	3:03	3:07

VO2:		38.9	38.0	37.2	36.4	35.6	34.8	34.0
2mi	race	17:25	17:49	18:13	18:38	19:03	19:28	19:55
		8:42	8:54	9:06	9:19	9:31	9:44	9:57
		2:10	2:13	2:16	2:19	2:22	2:26	2:29
5km	race	27:55	28:33	29:11	29:51	30:31	31:12	31:54
		8:59	9:11	9:23	9:36	9:49	10:02	10:16
		2:14	2:17	2:20	2:24	2:27	2:30	2:34
5mi	race	46:27	47:30	48:34	49:40	50:47	51:55	53:05
		9:17	9:30	9:42	9:56	10:09	10:23	10:37
		2:19	2:22	2:25	2:29	2:32	2:35	2:39
10km	race	58:37	59:56	1:01:17	1:02:40	1:04:05	1:05:31	1:07:00
		9:26	9:38	9:51	10:05	10:18	10:32	10:46
		2:21	2:24	2:27	2:31	2:34	2:38	2:41
15km	race	1:30:28	1:32:30	1:34:35	1:36:43	1:38:53	1:41:07	1:43:23
		9:42	9:55	10:08	10:22	10:36	10:50	11:05
		2:25	2:28	2:32	2:35	2:39	2:42	2:46
10mi	race	1:37:32	1:39:44	1:41:59	1:44:16	1:46:37	1:49:01	1:51:28
		9:45	9:58	10:11	10:25	10:39	10:54	11:08
		2:26	2:29	2:32	2:36	2:39	2:43	2:47
20km	race	2:03:05	2:05:51	2:08:41	2:11:35	2:14:32	2:17:34	2:20:40
		9:54	10:07	10:21	10:35	10:49	11:04	11:19
		2:28	2:31	2:35	2:38	2:42	2:46	2:49
13.1mi	race	2:10:19	2:13:15	2:16:15	2:19:19	2:22:27	2:25:39	2:28:56
		9:56	10:09	10:23	10:37	10:51	11:06	11:21
		2:29	2:32	2:35	2:39	2:42	2:46	2:50
25km	race	2:36:16	2:39:47	2:43:23	2:47:04	2:50:49	2:54:40	2:58:36
		10:03	10:17	10:31	10:45	10:59	11:14	11:29
		2:30	2:34	2:37	2:41	2:44	2:48	2:52
30km	race	3:09:56	3:14:13	3:18:35	3:23:03	3:27:37	3:32:17	3:37:04
		10:11	10:25	10:39	10:53	11:08	11:23	11:38
		2:32	2:36	2:39	2:43	2:47	2:50	2:54
Marthn	race	4:33:36	4:39:46	4:46:04	4:52:30	4:59:05	5:05:48	5:12:41
		10:26	10:40	10:54	11:09	11:24	11:39	11:55
		2:36	2:40	2:43	2:47	2:51	2:54	2:58
< 6mi	train	1:10:35	1:12:10	1:13:48	1:15:27	1:17:09	1:18:53	1:20:40
		11:45	12:01	12:18	12:34	12:51	13:08	13:26
		2:56	3:00	3:04	3:08	3:12	3:17	3:21
10mi	train	2:01:55	2:04:40	2:07:28	2:10:20	2:13:16	2:16:16	2:19:20
		12:11	12:28	12:44	13:02	13:19	13:37	13:56
		3:02	3:07	3:11	3:15	3:19	3:24	3:29
15mi	train	3:08:09	3:12:23	3:16:43	3:21:09	3:25:40	3:30:18	3:35:02
		12:32	12:49	13:06	13:24	13:42	14:01	14:20
		3:08	3:12	3:16	3:21	3:25	3:30	3:35
20mi	train	4:15:59	4:21:44	4:27:38	4:33:39	4:39:48	4:46:06	4:52:32
		12:47	13:05	13:22	13:40	13:59	14:18	14:37
		3:11	3:16	3:20	3:25	3:29	3:34	3:39

VO2:		33.3	32.6	31.8	31.1	30.5	29.8	29.1
2mi	race	20:22	20:49	21:17	21:46	22:15	22:45	23:16
		10:11	10:24	10:38	10:53	11:07	11:22	11:38
		2:32	2:36	2:39	2:43	2:46	2:50	2:54
5km	race	32:37	33:22	34:07	34:53	35:40	36:28	37:17
		10:30	10:44	10:58	11:13	11:28	11:44	12:00
		2:37	2:41	2:44	2:48	2:52	2:56	3:00
5mi	race	54:17	55:30	56:45	58:02	59:20	1:00:40	1:02:02
		10:51	11:06	11:21	11:36	11:52	12:08	12:24
		2:42	2:46	2:50	2:54	2:58	3:02	3:06
10km	race	1:08:30	1:10:03	1:11:37	1:13:14	1:14:53	1:16:34	1:18:17
		11:01	11:16	11:31	11:47	12:03	12:19	12:35
		2:45	2:49	2:52	2:56	3:00	3:04	3:08
15km	race	1:45:43	1:48:06	1:50:32	1:53:01	1:55:33	1:58:09	2:00:49
		11:20	11:35	11:51	12:07	12:23	12:40	12:57
		2:50	2:53	2:57	3:01	3:05	3:10	3:14
10mi	race	1:53:59	1:56:32	1:59:10	2:01:51	2:04:35	2:07:23	2:10:15
		11:23	11:39	11:55	12:11	12:27	12:44	13:01
		2:50	2:54	2:58	3:02	3:06	3:11	3:15
20km	race	2:23:49	2:27:04	2:30:22	2:33:45	2:37:13	2:40:45	2:44:22
		11:34	11:50	12:05	12:22	12:39	12:56	13:13
		2:53	2:57	3:01	3:05	3:09	3:14	3:18
13.1mi	race	2:32:17	2:35:43	2:39:13	2:42:48	2:46:28	2:50:12	2:54:02
		11:36	11:52	12:08	12:25	12:41	12:59	13:16
		2:54	2:58	3:02	3:06	3:10	3:14	3:19
25km	race	3:02:37	3:06:43	3:10:55	3:15:13	3:19:37	3:24:06	3:28:42
		11:45	12:01	12:17	12:34	12:50	13:08	13:26
		2:56	3:00	3:04	3:08	3:12	3:17	3:21
30km	race	3:41:57	3:46:57	3:52:03	3:57:16	4:02:37	4:08:04	4:13:39
		11:54	12:10	12:26	12:43	13:00	13:18	13:36
		2:58	3:02	3:06	3:10	3:15	3:19	3:24
Marthn	race	5:19:43	5:26:55	5:34:16	5:41:48	5:49:29	5:57:21	6:05:23
		12:11	12:28	12:44	13:02	13:19	13:37	13:56
		3:02	3:07	3:11	3:15	3:19	3:24	3:29
< 6mi	train	1:22:29	1:24:20	1:26:14	1:28:10	1:30:09	1:32:11	1:34:16
		13:44	14:03	14:22	14:41	15:01	15:21	15:42
		3:26	3:30	3:35	3:40	3:45	3:50	3:55
10mi	train	2:22:28	2:25:41	2:28:57	2:32:18	2:35:44	2:39:14	2:42:49
		14:14	14:34	14:53	15:13	15:34	15:55	16:16
		3:33	3:38	3:43	3:48	3:53	3:58	4:04
15mi	train	3:39:52	3:44:49	3:49:52	3:55:03	4:00:20	4:05:44	4:11:16
		14:39	14:59	15:19	15:40	16:01	16:22	16:45
		3:39	3:44	3:49	3:55	4:00	4:05	4:11
20mi	train	4:59:07	5:05:51	5:12:44	5:19:46	5:26:58	5:34:19	5:41:51
		14:57	15:17	15:38	15:59	16:20	16:42	17:05
		3:44	3:49	3:54	3:59	4:05	4:10	4:16

Heart Rate Tables

The following pages contain tables of running heart rates for various race and training distances. Each column represents a constant level of ability over various distances for a runner. Thus all a runner's race and training heart rates should theoretically appear in the same column. Each column in the tables going to the right represents approximately a 2% decrease in heart rate reserve. The numbers on the top line of the table are ages which can be used to estimate maximum heart rate given by the 2 mi race heart rate below the age in the table. These correspond to 220 – age.

Using the table:

- The first thing to do is to find your maximum heart rate in the table. This can be done by using the age on the top line, by finding your maximum heart rate measured by some other means in the 2 mi race heart rate row or by measuring your average heart rate during a race and finding the column that has a corresponding heart rate listed for the same race distance.

Using the table for racing:

- Within your column are estimated target average heart rates for any race distances listed.

Using the table for training:

- At the bottom of your column highlighted in light gray are easy, (80% effort), running heart rate targets for various endurance training runs. These heart rates are appropriate for base building runs and on easy days.

- The upper two (race) sections of your column highlighted in medium and light gray are running paces which are appropriate for interval or pace training at different race intensities.

Heart rates for interval or pace runs shorter than 800 meters are not useful for training targets since it takes at least that long for heart rate to stabilize.

AGE:	15	18	21	24	27	30	33
2mi race	205	201	198	195	192	190	187
5km race	200	197	194	191	188	185	183
5mi race	195	192	189	186	184	181	178
10km race	193	190	187	184	182	179	176
15km race	189	186	183	180	178	175	173
10mi race	188	185	183	180	177	175	172
20km race	186	183	180	178	175	173	170
13.1mi race	185	183	180	177	175	172	170
25km race	184	181	178	176	173	171	168
30km race	182	179	177	174	172	169	167
Marthn race	179	176	174	171	169	167	164
< 6mi train	164	162	160	158	155	153	151
10mi train	160	158	156	154	152	150	148
15mi train	157	155	153	151	149	147	145
20mi train	155	153	151	149	147	145	143

AGE:		35	38	41	43	46	48	51
2mi	race	184	181	179	176	174	171	169
5km	race	180	177	175	172	170	167	165
5mi	race	176	173	171	168	166	164	161
10km	race	174	171	169	166	164	162	160
15km	race	170	168	166	163	161	159	157
10mi	race	170	167	165	163	160	158	156
20km	race	168	166	163	161	159	157	154
13.1mi	race	167	165	163	161	158	156	154
25km	race	166	164	161	159	157	155	153
30km	race	165	162	160	158	156	154	151
Marthn	race	162	160	157	155	153	151	149
< 6mi	train	149	147	145	143	141	140	138
10mi	train	146	144	142	140	138	136	135
15mi	train	143	141	139	137	136	134	132
20mi	train	141	139	137	136	134	132	131

AGE:		53	56	58	60	62	64	67
2mi	race	166	164	162	159	157	155	153
5km	race	163	161	158	156	154	152	150
5mi	race	159	157	155	153	151	149	147
10km	race	157	155	153	151	149	147	145
15km	race	154	152	150	148	146	144	142
10mi	race	154	152	150	148	146	144	142
20km	race	152	150	148	146	144	142	141
13.1mi	race	152	150	148	146	144	142	140
25km	race	151	149	147	145	143	141	139
30km	race	149	147	145	144	142	140	138
Marthn	race	147	145	143	141	139	138	136
< 6mi	train	136	134	133	131	129	128	126
10mi	train	133	131	130	128	127	125	123
15mi	train	131	129	127	126	124	123	121
20mi	train	129	127	126	124	123	121	120

AGE:	69	71	73	75	76	78	80
2mi race	151	149	147	145	143	141	139
5km race	148	146	144	142	140	138	137
5mi race	145	143	141	139	137	135	134
10km race	143	141	139	138	136	134	132
15km race	141	139	137	135	133	132	130
10mi race	140	138	137	135	133	131	130
20km race	139	137	135	133	132	130	129
13.1mi race	138	137	135	133	132	130	128
25km race	137	136	134	132	131	129	127
30km race	136	135	133	131	130	128	126
Marthn race	134	132	131	129	128	126	125
< 6mi train	125	123	122	120	119	117	116
10mi train	122	121	119	118	116	115	114
15mi train	120	119	117	116	114	113	112
20mi train	119	117	116	114	113	112	111

References

Bandura, A. "Self-Reinforcement Process" in Self-Control: Power to the Person (M.J. Mahoney & C.E. Thoreson, eds.) Brooks/Cole Publishing Co., Monteray, Ca. 1974, pp. 86-110.

Bell, Jenna A' "Top Ten Sports Nutrition and Diet Questions" Sports, Cardiovascular and Wellness Nutrition" www.scandpg.com

Bobbert, Maarten F, Hollander, A. P. & Huijing, P. A. "Factors in Delayed Onset Muscular Soreness of Man" Medicine and Science in Sports and Exercise (18:1) 1986, pp. 75-81.

Brody, Jane Jane Brody's Nutrition Book Bantam Books, New York, New York, 1982.

Coleman, Ellen Eating For Endurance Roubidoux Printing Co., Riverside Ca., 1980.

Costill, David L., Ph. D. A Scientific Approach to Distance Running Track & Field News, 1979.

Daniels, J., Fitts, R. & Sheehan, G. Conditioning for Distance Running, The Scientific Aspects John Wiley & Son, New York, 1978.

Daws, Ron Running Your Best The Stephen Greene Press, Lexington, Massachusetts, 1985.

Finke, P. "Back to Basics" Series in The Oregon Distance Runner Winter, Spring & Summer 1984.

Forgac, M.T. "Carbohydrate Loading: A Review" Journal of the American Dietetic Association (75) July, 1979, pp. 42-45.

Garfield, Charles A., Ph.D. & Bennett, H.Z. Peak Performance Jeremy P. Tarcher, Inc., Los Angeles 1984.

Garfield, Charles A., Ph.D. "On Vitamins, Carboloading & Competition" Womens Sports & Fitness (7:9) October 1985.

Hamilton, Janet Running Strong &Injury Free Running Strong Publications Atlanta, 2000

Hartung, G.H. & Squires, W.G. "Physiologic Measures & Marathon Running Performance in Young & Middle Aged Runners" Journal of Sports Medicine (22) 1982, pp. 366-370.

Higdon, H. "Shadows on the Wall" The Runner November 1981, pp. 46, 50, 80-81.

Jones, D., Round, J., deHaan, A., Skeletal Muscle from Molecules to Movement, Churchill Livingdtone 2004

Kraus,W., "Skeletal Muscle Adaptation to Chronic Low-Frequency Motor Nerve Stimulation, Exercise Sport Science Review 1994, 22:213

Macek, M. & Vavia, J. "FIMS Position Statement on Training and Competition in Children" The Journal of Sports Medicine and Physical Fitness (20:2) 1980, pp 135-138.

Martin, W.H.3rd et al, "Effect of Endurance Training on Free Fatty Acid Turnover and Oxidation during Exercise", Endocrinology and Metabolism,265:E, pp 708-714

McArdle, W.D., Katch, F.I. & Katch, V.L. Exercise Physiology. Nutrition, Energy & Human Performance Lippincot Williams & Wilkins 7th edition, 2009

Millman, Dan The Warrior Athlete : Body Mind & Spirit Stillpoint Publishing, Walpole, New Hampshire 1979.

Moore, M. "Carbohydrate Loading: Eating through the Wall" The Physician & Sportsmedicine (9) October 1981, pp. 97-102.

Noakes, Tim, Lore of Running, Human Kinetics Champaign Ill, 2003

Orlick, Terry In Pursuit of Excellence Human Kinetics Publishers, Champaign, Ill., 1982.

Overfield, J.H. "Marathoning's Glorious Birth" Marathoner Winter 1979, pp.22-25.

Potera, Carol "The Running Body" Running Times November, 1985.

Romjin, J.A., "Regulation of Endogenous Fat and Carbohydrate Metabolism in Relation to Exercise Intensity and Duration" Journal of Applied Physiology 1993, pp380-391

Runner's Training Guide Runner's World Magazine, 1973.

"Secrets of Lactate" www.lactate.com

Shetlock, Frank G. & Prentice, W. E. "Warming Up and Stretching for Improved Physical Performance and Prevention of Sports-Related Injuries" Sports Medicine (2) 1985, pp. 267-278.

Sjodin, Bertil & Svedenhag, J. "Applied Physiology of Marathon Running" Sports Medicine (2) 1985, pp. 83-99

Tucker, Ross "The Mystery of Fatigue and the Limits to performance". www.sportsscientists.com

van der Beek, E. J. "Vitamins and Endurance Training" Sports Medicine (2) 1985, pp 175- 197.

Williams, M.H, Anderson, D., Rawson, E. Nutrition for Health Fitness & Sport McGraw Hill Higher Education, NY, NY, 10th Ed 2012

Wilmore, J.H. , Costill, D., Training for Sport & Activity. The Physiological Basis of the Conditioning Process Allyn & Bacon, Inc., 1993

Wischnia, B. "The Elements of Style" Runner's World December 1982, pp. 55-62.

About This Book

This book was originally written for the Portland Marathon Clinic, which we have been fortunate to have conducted since 1984.

The marathon clinic has provided thousands of runners with their first marathon experience, something nobody ever forgets. This book has been the basis of their training.

The clinics, and the Portland Marathon, are among the most successful in the United States.

The Authors

Patti and Warren Finke are co-directors of the Portland Marathon Clinic, a six month program of educational lectures and training runs leading to the Portland Marathon. Warren and Patti have been active in running clinics, seminars and publications since the late 1970s. Both are certified coaches with the Road Runners' Club of America. Patti and Warren developed and managed certification classes for the RRCA where they certified over 2000 running coaches.

Patti, an exercise physiologist and corporate fitness consultant, has used running to overcome chronic asthma. She has run over 85 marathons winning one women's title, placing in the top three in several others and winning many age group awards. She is an active ultrarunner completing over 85 and has held U.S. age records at 50 kilometers and 50 miles. Warren, a nationally ranked masters runner, has completed over 85 marathons winning three overall and eight masters titles. He placed third in the 1982 TAC US Masters Marathon Championship and was second veteran in the 1992 Boston Marathon. He is best known however, as an ultramarathoner having completed more than 85 races between 50 kilometers and 100 miles, winning 20 of them. He has twice held the U.S. open track record for 100 kilometers.

The Illustrator
Illustrations in this book were done by Clive Davies who at age 70 won the 1985 national age graded master's competition at the Twin Cities Marathon. Davies who began competing at age 57, set over 30 world age group records and had a personal best of 2:42 in the marathon at age 65.

Made in the USA
San Bernardino, CA
02 April 2016